# Sound Patterns of Spoken English

Chapter 1 begins by noting that most people aren't aware of the sounds of language. This book is written by one of those annoying people who listen not to what others say, but to how they say it. I dedicate it to fellow sound anoraks and to others interested in spoken language, with a hope that they will find it useful.

# Sound Patterns of
# Spoken English

*Linda Shockey*

 **Blackwell**
Publishing

350 Main Street, Malden, MA 02148-5018, USA
108 Cowley Road, Oxford OX4 1JF, UK
550 Swanston Street, Carlton South, Melbourne,
Victoria 3053, Australia
Kurfürstendamm 57, 10707 Berlin, Germany

First published 2003 by Blackwell Publishing Ltd

*Library of Congress Cataloging-in-Publication Data*

Shockey, Linda.
    Sound patterns of spoken English / Linda Shockey.
        p.   cm.
    Includes bibliographical references (p. ) and index.
    ISBN 0-631-23079-3 (hardcover : alk. paper) – ISBN 0-631-23080-7
(pbk. : alk. paper)
    1. English language – Phonology.   2. English language – Spoken
English.   3. English language – Variation.   4. Speech acts
(Linguistics)   5. Conversation.   I. Title.
    PE1133 .S47 2003
    421'.5 – dc21

                                                    2002007301

A catalogue record for this title is available from the British Library.

Set in 10/12.5pt
by Graphicraft Limited, Hong Kong
Printed and bound in the United Kingdom
by MPG Books Ltd, Bodmin, Cornwall

For further information on
Blackwell Publishing, visit our website:
http://www.blackwellpublishing.com

# Contents

# Figures and Tables

# *Preface*

This is not an introductory book: to get the most from it, a reader should have studied some linguistics and should therefore know the basics of phonetics and phonology. There are numerous works where these basics are presented clearly and knowledgeably, and it would be an unneccessary duplication of effort (as well as an embarrassing display of hubris) to attempt a recapitulation of what is known.

The following books (or others of a similar nature) should be assimilated before reading *Sound Patterns of Spoken English*:

Clark, J. and Yallop, C., *Introduction to Phonetics and Phonology*, Blackwell, 1995.
Ladefoged, P., *Vowels and Consonants*, Blackwell, 2000.
Roca, I. and Johnson, W., *A Course in Phonology*, Blackwell, 1999.

There are hundreds of other useful references included in the text of this book. A few of these which have formed my approach to the study of sounds (and to the authors of which I am greatly indebted) follow:

Bailey, C.-J., *New Ways of Analysing Variation in English*, Georgetown University Press, 1973.
Brown, G., *Listening to Spoken English*, Longman, 1977, 1996.
Hooper, J., *Natural Generative Phonology*, Academic Press, 1976.

Lehiste, I., *Suprasegmentals*, MIT Press, 1970.
Stampe, D., *A Dissertation on Natural Phonology*, Garland, 1979.

In my opinion, these works show great insight into the study of spoken language.

# 1

# *Setting the Stage*

Most people speaking their native language do not notice either the sounds that they produce or the sounds that they hear. They focus directly on the meaning of the input and output: the sounds serve as a channel for the information, but not as a focus in themselves (cf. Brown 1977: 4–5) This is obviously the most efficient way to communicate. If we were to allow a preoccupation with sounds to get in the way of understanding, we would seriously handicap our interactions. One consequence of this opacity of the sound medium is that our notion of how we pronounce words and longer utterances can be very different from what we actually say.

Take a sentence like 'And the suspicious cases were excluded.' Whereas a speaker of English might well think they are saying:

(a)  ændðəsəs'pɪʃəskeɪsɨzwəɹɛks'kludɨd

what they may be producing is

(b)  ŋəs:'pɪʂkeɪsɨsə<sup>w</sup>xs'kludɨt

This book will look how you get from (a) to (b). It deals with pronunciation as found in everyday speech – i.e. normal pronunciation. Years of listening closely to English as spoken by people from a great variety of groups (age, sex, status, geographic origin, education) leads me to believe that there are some phonological differences from citation form which occur in many types of spoken English. Further, these differences are very common within these varieties of English and fall into easily recognizable types which can be described using a small number of phonological processes, most of which can be seen to operate in English under other circumstances.

I call these differences 'reductions' (though this term is a loose one: sometimes characteristics are added or simply changed rather than lost). A citation form is the most formal pronunciation used by a particular person. It can be different for different people: for example, the most formal form of the word 'celery' has three syllables for some people and two syllables for others. For the former group, the pronunciation ['sɛlɹi] involves a reduction, for the latter group, it does not.

['sɛlɹi] could, however, have been a reduced form in the history of the language of the two-syllable group, even if not within the lifetime of current speakers. That it is no longer a reduced form attests to its 'promotion': the word is pronounced in its reduced form so often that the reduced form becomes standard. I speak as if promotion occurs to individual lexical items rather than classes of items, because it can be shown that not all words which have a given structure will undergo reduction and promotion: 'raillery', for example, will presumably remain a three-syllable word for those who have only two in 'celery', perhaps because the former is an unusual word, perhaps because it has more internal structure than 'celery' perhaps for other reasons. In general, the more common an item is, the more likely it is to reduce, given that it contains elements which are reduction-prone (see chapter 2).

The idea of lexeme-specific phonology is not a new one: many phonologists and sociolinguists have worked under the assumption that phonological change over time occurs first in a single word or small set of words, then spreads to a larger set – what is known as 'lexical diffusion'. (For an early treatment, see Wang, 1977.)

The citation form is therefore not the same as a phonological underlying form: it must be pronounceable and will appear as such in a pronouncing dictionary. Words like 'celery' generally appear with both pronunciations cited above.

Deciding what is a reduced form can hence be difficult, but there are few debatable cases in the material I present here: nearly every native speaker of English will agree that the word 'first' has a /t/ at the end in citation form, but virtually none of them will pronounce it under certain conditions.

The material which I cover in this treatise overlaps the boundaries of several areas of study: sociolinguistics, for example, is interested in which reductions are used most frequently by given groups and what social forces spark them off. Lexicography may be interested in reduced variants, but only in so far as they are found in words in isolation, whereas this work looks at reductions very much in terms of the stream of speech in which they occur. Rhetoricians or singing teachers may regard reductions as dangerous deviations from maximal intelligibility, and a similar attitude may be found in speech scientists attempting to do automatic speech recognition. This book recognizes reductions as a normal part of speech and further suggests that the forces which cause them in English are the same forces which result in most-favoured output in others of the world's languages.

## 1.1   Phonetics or Phonology?

It has been demonstrated (Lieberman, 1970; Fowler and Housum, 1987; Fowler, 1988) that there is *phonetic reduction* in connected speech, especially in words which have once been focal but have since passed to a lower information status: the first time a word is used, its articulation is more precise and the resulting acoustic signal more distinct than in subsequent tokens of the same word. By 'phonetic' I mean that the effect can be described in terms of of vocal tract inertia: since the topic is known, it is not necessary to make the effort to achieve a maximal pronunciation after the first token. We expect the same to happen in all languages, though there may be differences of degree.

Phonetic effects are not the only ones which one finds in relaxed, connected speech: there are also language-specific reductions which occur in predictable environments and which appear to be controlled by cognitive mechanisms rather than by physical ones. These we term phonological reductions because they are part of the linguistic plan of a particular language. Sotillo (1997) has shown that these behave quite differently from the phonetic effects described above: whereas phonetic effects are sensitive to previous mention, phonological reductions are not.

We speak here as if phonetics and phonology were distinct disciplines, and some feel confident in assigning a given 'phonomenon' to one or the other (Keating, 1988; Farnetani and Recasens, 1996). Both comprise the study of sounds, but can this study be divided into two neat sections?

'Phonology' has meant different things to different people over the course of the history of linguistics. Looking at it logically, what are possible meanings for the term, given that it has to mean 'something more abstract than phonetics'?

(1)   One could take the stance that phonology deals only with the relationship between sound units in a language (segmental and suprasegmental) and meaning (provided you are referring to lexical rather than indexical meaning). Truly phonological events would then involve exchanges of sound units which made a difference in meaning, either:
(a)   from meaning 1 to meaning 2 (e.g. pin/pan) or
(b)   from meaning 1 to non-meaning or vice versa (e.g. pan/pon).
Phonetics would be everything else and would deal with how these units are realized: all variation, conditioned or unconditioned would then be phonetics. As far as I know, this does not correspond to a position ever taken by a real school of phonology, but is a logical possibility.

(2)   Phonology could be seen as the study of meaning-changing sound units and their representatives in different environments, regardless of whether they change the meaning, and with no constraints on the relationship between the abstract phoneme and its representatives in speech: anything can change to anything else, as long as the change is regular/predictable, that is, as long as the linkage to the underlying phonemic identity of each item is discoverable. This will allow one-to-one, many-to-one, and one-to-many mappings between underlying components and surface components, as well as no mapping (in which an underlying component has no phonetic realization).

This type of phonology would look at the sound system of a language as an abstract code in which the identity of each element is determined entirely by its own original description and by its relationship to other elements. Fudge (1967) provides an early example of introducing phonological primes with no implicit phonetic content.

Foley's point of view (1977) is not unlike this: his thesis is that phonological elements can be identified only through their participation in phonological rules:

> As, for example, the elements of a psychological theory must be established without reduction to neurology or physiology, so too the elements of a phonological theory must be established by consideration of phonological processes, without reduction to the phonetic characteristics of the superficial elements. (p. 27)

and 'Only when phonology frees itself from phonetic reductionism will it attain scientific status.'

Kelly and Local (1989) also take a position of this sort: 'We draw a strict distinction between phonology and phonetics. Phonology is formal and to be treated in the algebraic domain; phonetics is physical and in the temporal domain.'

Any school which determines membership of a phonological class by distribution alone might be said to take a similar stance: de Saussure's analogy between phonological units and pieces in the game of chess could be interpreted this way.

(3) Phonology could be seen as the study of meaning-bearing sound units and their representatives in different environments, regardless of whether they change the meaning, with the addition of constraints as to what sorts of substitutions are likely or even possible.

If constraints are specified, phonology offers some insight into why changes take place, based on the articulatory and perceptual properties of the input and output. A congruous assumption is that since vocal tracts, ears, and brains are essentially the same in all humans, some aspects of phonology are universal.

Most currently-favoured phonological theories are like this: in Chomsky's terminology, they attempt to achieve explanatory as well as descriptive adequacy. Generative grammar opted to incorporate links between abstract phonology and the vocal tract through (1) a choice of features which reflect normal human articulatory possibilities and (2) 'parsimony' (the rule using the fewest features is best, hence rules involve small changes which are easily executed by the vocal tract). Linked to this are the 'natural classes': sounds which are articulated similarly are very likely to undergo similar phonological changes. Autosegmental phonology achieves a link with the vocal tract through structuring of feature lattices, gestural phonology through encoding phonological elements in terms of the articulators themselves. (These themes will be taken up in chapter 3.)

It is, of course, generally understood that articulatory involvement cannot always be presupposed by a theory because in some cases the physical motivation for a phonological event has become inadequate (Anderson, 1981). For example, the f/v alternation in singular/plural words (shelf/shelves, roof/rooves, loaf/loaves) is not currently productive (*Smurf/Smurves), though variation owing to this process is still part of the language. These remains of decommissioned processes are often called fossils. Or the alternation could be the result of an interaction with another linguistic level (cf. Kaisse, 1985) rather than having an articulatory origin. For example, in the utterance 'I have to wear what I have to wear', (meaning 'I must wear clothing which I own') the first 'have' can be pronounced [hæf] while the second cannot, for lexical/syntactic reasons.

These cases aside, when we look at motivated alternations, we begin to consider the relationship between abstract categories and human architecture: this could be seen as a small subset of the mind/body problem so beloved of philosophers.

Most theories of phonology assume that spoken language involves categories which exist only in the minds of the speakers and for which there is thought to be a set of templates: some for segmental categories, some for tones, intonation, and voice quality. Another assumption which is usually not overt is that in speech production, our goal is to articulate strings of perfect tokens of these categories, but are held back from doing so by either communicative or physical demands.

Again musing on logical possibilities, we can imagine several variations on mind–body interaction.

### 1.1.1 More mind than body (fossils again)

Some sequences take more attention than others, and some even take more attention than they are worth, because they do not contribute substantially to the understanding of the utterance. Over time, it becomes customary to simplify these forms through a kind of unspoken treaty amongst native speakers of a language. This leads to our not pronouncing, say the 't' in 'Christmas', the 'b' in 'bomb', or the 'gh' in 'knight'. Eventually, the base form starts to be learned as a whole, so that younger speakers of the language do not even know that, for example, 'bomb' has a potential 'b' at the end and find out only by learning to spell.

These changes, as mentioned above, are primarily matters of convention and history.

### 1.1.2 A 50/50 mixture

Articulatory ease is more evidently a cause for change in cases such as word-final devoicing, which occurs very often with English oral obstruents: one rarely encounters a fully voiced final fricative or stop, even in careful speech. This change from the base form has a different psychological status from the previous one, however: native speakers do not know they are devoicing, and new generations are not led to believe that final obstruents are voiceless, though they pick up the habit of devoicing, as they must in order to sound like native speakers. It is easy to find languages where this feature is an overt convention (e.g. the Slavic languages, German, Turkish). It seems that here we have a peaceful settlement between what the vocal tract wants and what the brain decides to do.

Many characteristics of spoken English seem to fall into this intermediate category. For example, in vowel + nasal sequences, it is not unusual to nasalize the vowel and to not execute the closure for the nasal consonant. This means that words like 'can't' can be realized as [kãt]. At the phonetic level, then, there can be a contrast between plain and nasalized vowels in words like 'cart' and 'can't'. While this is a full-fledged phonological process in languages like French and Portuguese, it is merely a tendency in English and Japanese: a habit which is picked up by native speakers and used subconsciously.

*British*

### 1.1.3  More body than mind

In other cases, vocal tract influences seem clear and inevitable, as in the fronting of velar consonants before front vowels. This is called 'coarticulation' and is a function of the fact that the vocal tract has to execute sequences in which commands can conflict ('front' for [i], 'back' for [k], and a compromise is reached. This seems to me a clear case of a phonetic process, but it also seems quite clear that it can have phonological consequences, as in Swedish, where the sequence (which was historically and which is still spelled) [ki] is pronounced [çi], or as in English alternations such as act/action.

Bladon and Al-Bamerni (1976) have also pointed out that *resistance* to coarticulation can occur as a result of other demands of a language. In English, [k] and [i] can coarticulate freely, since a fronted [k] is not likely to be misinterpreted. In languages with a [c], [k] has less freedom to move about. This indicates that even process which are largely controlled by the vocal tract can be moderated by cognitive processes.

Resistance to coarticulation can also develop for no obvious reason: in Catalan, there is virtually no nasalization of vowels before nasal consonants, though it is found in the other Romance languages. (Stampe (1979: 17) cites denasalization as a natural process, and we can see this at work elsewhere in Catalan: whereas Spanish has [mɑno] and Portuguese [mãũ] for 'hand,' Catalan has [mɑ], with a plain vowel.)

If we accept that our third definition of phonology is a reasonable one, how can we distinguish phonology from phonetics? What is the difference between saying that changes have to have an articulatory or perception explanation and saying that the vocal tract is *responsible* for the changes? What is the interaction between the physical demands of the vocal tract and the desire on the part of the speaker to (a) be intelligible and (b) sound like a native speaker?

The answer seems obvious: as long as constraints determined by the shape and movement of the vocal tract are included in one's phonology, there is in principle no way to draw a boundary between phonetics and phonology. Processes which are essentially phonetic (such as nasalization of vowels before nasal consonants) are prerequisites for certain phonological changes (lack of closure for the nasal consonant, leading to distinctiveness of the nasalized vowel). Distinctions which are essentially phonological (such as the word-final voicing contrast in English obstruents) are signalled by largely phonetic features such as duration of the preceding vowel (though, granted, this process is exaggerated in English beyond the purely phonetic). Language features which are said to be phonological are constantly in the process of becoming non-distinctive, while features said to be phonetic are in the process of becoming distinctive. There are obvious cases of truly phonological processes and truly phonetic ones, but between them there is a continuum rather than a definable cutoff point.

### 1.1.4 Functional phonology and perception

The discourse above has been largely couched in terms of the generation of variants. If we are to think of phonology as not just an output device, but also as a facility which allows us to use the sound system of our native language, we must also think of it in terms of perception. In this framework, we can ask how knowledge of variability in a sound system is acquired and used and we can explore the relationship of this knowledge to phonological theory: are the sound units used for perception the units we posit in a phonological analysis? These questions, while normally thought of as psycholinguistic ones, are clearly important for an understanding of casual speech phonology. We will go into this more deeply in the second half of chapter 3.

### 1.1.5   Have we captured the meaning of 'phonology'?

We have, rather, shown that there are many ways to define phonology. I propose a further one:

(4)   Phonology is the systematic study of the pronunciation/perception targets and processes used by native speakers of a language in everyday life. It presupposes articulatory control of not only the contrasts used meaningfully in a language, but also of other dynamic features which lead to variation in speech sounds, such as tension of the vocal tract walls (cf. Keating, 1988: 286). It therefore includes all articulatory choices which make a native speaker sound native, including sociolinguistic variables such as register and style. It does *not* include simple coarticulation but can place limits on degree of coarticulation (Farnetani and Recasens, 1995; Manuel, 1990; Whalen, 1990).

Note that here again, the boundary between phonetics and phonology is hard to define, though it is clear that version 4 phonology includes a great deal of what is normally thought of as phonetics.

*Stampe influence*

### 1.1.6   Influence of phonology on phonetics

We have suggested that phonetics 'works its way up' into phonology. It must also be recognized that phonology 'works its way down' into phonetics. We think of speech sounds as being representatives of abstract categories despite there being a very large number of ways that one realization of a phonological unit can differ from another realization of the same phonological unit. When we do phonetic transcription, we use essentially the same symbol to represent quite different variants because phonology guides our choice of symbols. We can avoid this to some extent when listening to a language we do not know, but once the basics of the new language are assimilated, phonological categorization again takes over. This process has been useful in helping us derive new spelling systems for previously unwritten languages, but stands in the way of our experiencing phonetic events phonetically. The very notion that connected speech can be divided up into segments and represented

*Do people trip over phonetics/phonology because the question is wrong?*

with discrete symbols is a phonological one, reinforced by our alphabetic writing system.

### 1.1.7   Back to basics

Let us now return to the question of whether this book is about phonetics or phonology. In the light of what was said above, it is not clear that this question needs to be answered, or even that it is a meaningful question. By definitions 1 and 2, most of the material covered here will have to be thought of as phonetics. By definitions 3 and 4, it is mainly phonology. Suffice it to say that it deals with systematic behaviour by native speakers (of English in this case, though not in principle) using fluent speech in everyday communicative situations.

## 1.2   Fast Speech?

Casual speech processes are often referred to as 'fast speech rules'. Results are not yet conclusive about whether increase in speech rate increases the amount of phonological reduction: it seems clear that phonetic undershoot takes place as less time is available for each linguistic unit, but evidence cited below suggests that cognitive factors are more important than inertia, despite the fact that connected speech processes are often called 'fast speech rules'.

A commonsense view of connected speech has it that the vocal tract is like any other machine: as you run it faster, it has to cut corners, so the gestures get less and less extreme. Say, for example, you are tracing circles in the air with your index finger. At a rate of one a second, you can draw enormous circles but if you're asked to do 6 per second, you have to draw much smaller circles, and a rate of 15 per second is impossible, no matter how small they are. So if you try to do 15, you might get only 10 – effectively, 5 have dropped out.

The same reasoning is applied to the vocal tract: as you execute targets faster and faster, the gestures become smaller and smaller, and sometimes they have to drop out entirely, which is why you get deletions in so-called 'fast speech'.

A moment's thought will convince you that the analogy here is not very good: the vocal tract is a very complicated device, and different parts of it can move simultaneously. The elements which comprise the vocal tract are of different sizes and shapes and have different degrees of mobility. The speech units which are being produced are very different from each other. And, most importantly, speech is not just an activity, it is a means of communication. This means that different messages will be transmitted nearly each time a person speaks, different units will be executed in sequence, and different conditions will be in effect to constrain articulation. For example, one can speak to a person who is very close or very far away, to a skilled or unskilled user of the language, with or without background noise.

The 'finger circle' analogy also does not take into account the relationship between the higher centres of the brain and articulation. Speech is a skill which we practise from infancy and one over which we have great control: does it seem likely that anyone would run their vocal tract so fast that not all of the sounds in a message could be executed? One might imagine singing a song so fast that not all of the notes/words could be included: the difference here is that we are executing a pre-established set of targets with a fixed internal rhythm *intended* for performance at a certain speed. But presumably, in real speech, our output is tailored to the situation in which it is uttered and has no such constraints.

Another argument against our very simplistic view of 'fast speech deletion' is that there are very distinct patterns of reduction in connected speech, related to type of sound and place of occurrence. If one were simply speaking too fast to include all the segments in a message, would not the last few simply drop out, as with our 'finger circles'? Rather, we find specific types of sounds being under-executed, in predictable locations. And these 'shortcuts' are different from language to language as well. Surely the importance of cognitive control of these mechanisms cannot be underrated.

Lindblom (1990) follows this line of reasoning in his 'H&H theory' of speech, which essentially says that in any given situation, the vocal tract will move as little as possible, provided that (situationally-determined) intelligibility can be maintained. This theory thus predicts a limit to the degree of undershoot based on the communicative demands of the moment.

*right*

While this point of view has a lot to be said for it, it cannot be considered a phonetic or phonological theory exclusively: it embraces all areas of linguistics, because they all contribute to the 'communicative demands of the moment'. Take an example from one of my recorded interviews: the speaker said [soʃ ʂˈkɚɾi] 'social security'. The underarticulation of this phrase is allowed because of discourse features (the topic is 'welfare mothers') and other pragmatic features (social security has been mentioned previously) as well as because of the syllable shapes and stress patterns involved. While the interests of the articulators are served by the apparent disappearance of certain sounds, the articulators cannot be said to have caused the underarticulation.

Finally, it is obvious that the types of reduction which we have been looking at also occur in slow speech: if you say 'eggs and bacon' slowly, you will probably still pronounce 'and' as [m], because it is conventional – that is, your output is being determined by habit rather than by speed or inertia. This brings us back full circle to the question 'phonetics or phonology?' Habit and convention are language-specific and are part of the underlying language plan rather than part of moment-to-moment movement of the articulators. Habits of pronunciation are systematic and predictable and can be linked only indirectly to articulator inertia.

## 1.3   Summary

This book is about the differences from citation form pronunciation which occur in conversational English and their perceptual consequences. We call these changes 'phonological' because they systematically occur only to certain sounds and in certain parts of words and syllables and because they are different from connected speech processes in other languages. Hence, they form part of the abstract pattern of pronunciation which is the competence of the native speaker. While they reflect constraints in the vocal tract, they are not purely phonetic: the boundary between phonetic and phonological processes is indistinct and probably undiscoverable given present-day notions of phonology. The reductions found in unselfconscious speech cannot legitimately be called 'fast speech' processes.

# 2

# *Processes in Conversational English*

The phonology of casual English should be thought of as dynamic and distributed. By the former, I mean that the processes which apply are very much a product of the moment and not entirely predictable: sometimes a process which seems likely to apply does not, and sometimes processes apply in surprising circumstances.

By the latter, I mean that the causes of a reduction are not only phonological but can be attributed to a wide range of linguistic sources. Conversational speech processes are partially conditioned by the phonetic nature of surrounding segments, but other factors such as stress, timing, syllable structure and higher-level discourse effects play a part in nearly every case. In the material which follows, I pass briefly over little-researched sources of phonological variability (a–c in table 2.1) and focus on those for which more information is available.

## 2.1   The Vulnerability Hierarchy

The chart in table 2.1 summarizes the influences which I have found to be most explanatory of casual speech reduction.

### 2.1.1   Frequency

In general, the more common an item is, the more likely it is to reduce, given that it contains elements which are reduction-prone

*Table 2.1* Factors influencing casual speech reduction

|  | Low reduction | High reduction |
| --- | --- | --- |
| **(a) Frequency** | infrequent | frequent |
| **(b) Discourse** | | |
| Focus | focal | non- or defocal |
| Prescription | prescriptive | unnoticed |
| Medium | scripted | unscripted |
| **(c) Rate?** | slow? | fast? |
| **(d) Function in larger linguistic unit** | | |
| Stress | stressed | unstressed |
| Place in word | beginning | end |
| Place in syllable | beginning | end |
| Part of speech | content | function (short, frequent) |
| **(e) Phonetic/Phonological** | | |
| Environment | non-cluster | cluster |
| Place of articulation | non-alveolar | alveolar |
|  | non-ð | ð |

Incredibly vulnerable: [t], [ð], [ə]
Moderately vulnerable: /n/, /d/, /l/, /z/
Practically invulnerable: /f/, /m/, /ʃ/, /tʃ/, /dʒ/

| **(f) Morphological** | | |
| --- | --- | --- |
|  | gerund | present participle |
|  | polymorphemic | monomorphemic |

(see my comments on 'celery' in chapter 1). Greenberg and Fosler-Lussier (2000) have observed this tendency in a large digitized corpus of American English. They link it to the observation that the brain appears to process words of high frequency more quickly than their infrequent counterparts (p. 3, and (their citation) Howes, 1967), hypothesizing that therefore frequent words may need to be less fully specified in order to achieve adequate communication.

## 2.1.2 Discourse

Discourse features are not being highlighted here because very little has been written about the effects of discourse on conversational phonology.

Broadly speaking, English is a topic-comment language, i.e. the old information comes first, followed by the new. There is also a strong tendency for the beginnings of utterances to be spoken faster and, impressionistically speaking, less carefully than the ends: phrase- and sentence-final lengthening are regarded as unquestionable features of English, and it would not be unreasonable to expect more phonological reduction in the 'topic' portion of an utterance than in the 'comment' portion.

One study (Shockey, Spelman Miller and Wichmann, 1994) used the Functional approach (Firbas, 1992) to mark spontaneous text and then looked at the correlation between function and phonological reduction. No correlation could be found, but we were left with the feeling that our procedure for marking focus had not been appropriate, since it was developed for written language and sometimes had to be stretched to cover the data. We think therefore that the development of a model which links function and phonological reduction is a viable project.

It has been shown that first mentions or focal mentions of any particular lexical item will be more fully articulated than subsequent tokens of the same word. Lieberman (1970) and Fowler and Housum (1987) have certainly found this to be the case for phonetic features of speech: subsequent mentions show more acoustic-phonetic undershoot than first uses. It has been shown many times over that speech taken from the middle of connected discourse is hard to understand on its own, (cf. Pickett and Pollack, 1963) presumably (at least partially) because the initial, clear tokens of the topic words are not available for comparison.

**Prescription** refers to whether a phonological process is thought by users to reflect vulgarity or lack of education. 'Dropping your aitches' or 'leaving out your g's' (as in readin' and writin') are known to be nonstandard by most speakers of English, so these processes are suppressed whenever there is fear of negative opinion.

Processes such as ð-assimilation receive no notice in the letters page of the *Daily Telegraph* or in primary education and therefore remain subconscious for nearly all speakers. Suppression of these is not known to happen: if you don't know you're doing something, you're not likely to try to stop.

**Medium** refers to whether the speaker is performing read or memorized speech (scripted speech), in which case the degree of reduction can be relatively low, or spontaneous (unscripted) speech, in which case reduction is likely, given the proper conditioning factors.

Degree of formality seems to have little effect on unscripted speech: one finds the same types and nearly the same number of reductions in formal English as one does in casual speech. Most texts on unselfconscious speech take the commonsense position that as the situation becomes less formal, speech becomes more 'sloppy'. But, based on my research, I have to claim that common sense is misguided in this case. There are differences in posture, gesture, and vocabulary choice, but little difference in phonological structure can be found. Since most connected speech phonology is subconscious, it is not changed in different styles. (cf. Brown, 1977: 55)

The impression that formal speech is less phonologically reduced than casual speech is probably based on the fact that much of (if not most) formal speech is scripted rather than spontaneous.

It is important to note that by 'style' here, we are not referring to a sociolect. There are certainly differences in pronunciation which go with changing reference group, and there is a vast body of literature on this subject. Here I am referring to changes which are likely to occur within a sociolect when comparing citation forms with spontaneous speech.

### 2.1.3 Rate?

Although it is often assumed that speaking fast leads to phonological reduction, the evidence is far from convincing (see chapter 1). Shockey (1987) suggests that fast rate is a sufficient cause for reduction, but not a necessary one.

### 2.1.4   Membership in a linguistic unit

Position in another linguistic unit can influence the behaviour of a speech segment: stressed syllables show less reduction than unstressed ones, word/syllable-initial consonants show less reduction than word/syllable-final ones.

Ongoing work (Vassière, 1988; Cooper, 1991; Dilley, Shattuck-Hufnagel and Ostendorf, 1996; Keating, 1997), suggests that consonants which begin larger prosodic units are even more fully pronounced than those which begin words: Fougeron and Keating (1997) report that within each prosodic domain (word, phrase, intonational phrase, utterance), [n] in initial CV syllables has greater articulatory contact (based on electropalatography (see chapter 4)) than [n] in medial and final CV syllables.

Syntactic function (part of speech) can be significant, but in interaction with other factors: short, frequent function words such as 'and' and 'of' are likely to show reduction, but function words such as 'hence', 'thereupon', 'moreover' and 'nevertheless' are not likely to. Pronouns normally show more reduction than nouns.

### 2.1.5   Phonetic/Phonological

The identity of the segment itself and its immediate phonetic/phonological environment can influence whether or not it undergoes reduction. Alveolars /t, d, n, l/ and to some extent the fricatives /s, z/ are particularly prone to change. It has been suggested (see chapter 3) that because English alveolars are so volatile, they are the unmarked underlying stop (Paradis and Prunet, 1989, 1991; Lodge, 1992; Lahiri and Marslen-Wilson, 1991).

Membership in a syllable- or word-final cluster increases the vulnerability of alveolar stops and nasals. When the final cluster is followed by one or more consonants in the next word, the vulnerability becomes even greater.

Voiced alveolar stops and nasals are also particularly prone to assimilation, often across a word or morpheme boundary. For example 'bad guy' can be pronounced as (something approximating) 'bag guy', 'pinball' as 'pimball', 'lane closure' as 'laing closure'. Claims for voiceless stop assimilations such as 'sweep boy' and

'sweek girl' (sweet boy/girl) (Cruttenden, 2001: 286; Marslen-
Wilson, Nix and Gaskell, 1995) are also made, but I think these
take only the oral gesture into account and do not acknowledge
the glottal component which is usually present in final voiceless
stops in this environment. Final alveolar fricatives are known to
assimilate to following postalveolars: 'this shop' [ðɪʃːɒp], 'cheese
shop' [ʧiːʒʃɒp] (Cruttenden, 2001: 285). These assimilations do
not particularly belong to casual speech and have been adequately
documented elsewhere, so will not be further pursued here.

Alveolar assimilation becomes interesting in casual speech when it
is combined with other processes, as when 'handbag' is pronounced
'hambag.' (See the final section of this chapter.)

The influence of membership in a linguistic unit and of phonetic/
phonological factors will be discussed below.

### 2.1.6 Morphological

The morphological class to which a word belongs can affect its
realization. My 1973 study showed, for example, that Central Ohio
residents produced [n] for [ŋ] in present participles of verbs (he's
seeing, going, doing) but not in gerunds (golfing, swimming, walk-
ing is his hobby). The most extensively studied case is undoubtedly
that of final t/d in monomorphemes (past, mist) and in morphologically complex items (passed, missed). All else being equal and
in all accents investigated, t/d is produced much less frequently in
the former than the latter (see Labov, 1997 for a review).

## 2.2 Reduction Processes in English

Experimental studies of several of these processes will be outlined
in the following sections.

### 2.2.1 Varieties examined

Two facts make my point: (1) there is an International Association
for World Englishes and (2) Wells' *Accents of English* (1982) runs to
three volumes. There are hundreds of varieties which can legitimately

be called English, and they differ in nearly every way possible: phonetically, phonologically, syntactically, pragmatically, etc. Recalling the sound of Indian, Caribbean, Singaporean and African English, it is easy to convince oneself that while many people from these areas are native speakers of English, they do not sound like each other nor like speakers of Standard Southern British and are hence likely to have very different conventions for casual speech. In this book, I have dealt with the varieties of English (1) about which I found the most published and (2) which I have worked with myself. These include General American, Australian, New Zealand, Southern Irish, Standard Southern British, and several local accents from the United Kingdom. Examples taken from Lodge (1984) are from Stockport (a suburb of Manchester), Coventry, Edinburgh, Norwich, Peasmarsh and Shepherd's Bush (part of West London). Some East London examples are also mentioned.

The map in figure 2.1 shows Lodge's research sites. It can be seen that they cover a great deal of ground. This is not to say that his work approaches a full coverage of English accents: these are simply a fair sample of them.

I regret that I was not able to include more accents in this work, and expect to hear that my generalizations do not apply to the many accents with which I am not familiar. The accents I have included have a similar rhythmic basis, and I suspect that accents which do not share this will diverge significantly from what I have found. The good news is that the field is still wide open for investigating conversational speech in these accents.

The following abbreviations are used below: Am. = General American, SSB. = Standard Southern British, ELon. = East London, Stkpt. = Stockport, Cov. = Coventry, Ed. = Edinburgh, Nor. = Norwich, Psmsh. = Peasmarsh and ShB. = Shepherd's Bush.

## 2.3   Stress as a Conditioning Factor

The varieties of English included in this book depend heavily on stress as a bearer of meaning. (It is said that English is a 'stress-timed language', and this impression is useful, even if it is only a metaphor.) Unstressed syllables in English tend to show reduced

*Figure 2.1*  Map of Lodge's research sites

vowels, as is universally known. But in conversational speech, unstressed syllables undergo other kinds of reduction as well.

### 2.3.1   Schwa absorption

I have adapted Wells' term 'schwa absorption' (1982: 434) to describe cases where something else in the vicinity of a schwa takes on its syllabic property but loses the openness of a vowel, i.e. whatever sound is left has the articulatory qualities of a consonant but the syllabic qualities of a vowel. (See also Wells, p. 286 'Syllabic Consonant Formation'.) There seem to be several different causes which 'conspire' (cf. Kisseberth, 1970 and see below on syllable shape) to this end, including overlap and vowel devoicing. ᔑ

It has long been an axiom of English phonology that certain sounds can be syllabic under the right circumstances. For example if the 't' is released nasally, the 'n' of 'cotton' is syllabic, if the 't' is released laterally, the 'l' of 'cattle' is syllabic.

The apparent loss of a schwa is thus commonplace, but the number of syllables in a word or phrase is typically preserved. It is as if the reduced vowel is simply a syllabic place holder, as its phonetic quality is largely determined by its environment (cf. Browman and Goldstein, 1992 and attendant comments; Bates, 1995). When something else can assume syllabicity, the schwa need not appear.

Syllabic resonants are normally considered to be reflexes of a sequence consisting of [ə] followed by a resonant. There are, however, cases of syllabicity being assumed by a number of consonants as well as voiceless vowels.

*Laterals*

| | |
|---|---|
| 'faɪnl̩i | Am. 'finally' |
| l̩'æskə | Am. 'Alaska' |
| ð'l̩ɛɪk | Am. 'the lake' |
| l̩æbɚət | Am. 'elaborate' |
| 'ɔːfl̩ | Stkpt. 'awful' |
| pipl̩n̩ | SSB. 'people and' |
| ʌnjuː3l̩ | Ed. 'unusual' |

| | |
|---|---|
| lĩʔɬ | Nor. 'little' |
| mɑːvɬəs | ShB. 'marvellous' |
| 'sɪvɬ | Ed. 'civil' |
| b'ɬoni | Am. 'baloney' |

Syllabic resonants can occur across notional word boundaries, as in 'a lot' [ɬɒt] and 'the lake' as above.

*Nasals*

**(predominantly alveolars)**

| | |
|---|---|
| 'θaʊzn̩ | Am. 'thousand' |
| 'ɹaɪʔn̩ | Am. 'right in' |
| 'gɛʔn̩ | Am. 'gotten' |
| n̩'u | Am. 'a new' |
| ɛːʔn̩ | Cov. 'out on' |
| wʊn̩ | ShB. 'wouldn't' |
| n̩ɛi | SSB. 'And they' |
| 'ʃonn̩ʔ | Stkpt. 'shouldn't' |
| gɛʔn̩oðə | Stkpt. 'get another' |
| 'steʃn̩ | Ed. 'station' |
| gon̩ | Ed. 'going' |
| ɹeːzn̩z | Nor. 'raisins' |
| n̩'nʌðə | Nor. 'another' |

**(non-alveolars)**

| | |
|---|---|
| 'oʊpm̩z | Nor. 'opens' |
| 'badm̩ | Psmsh. 'bottom' |
| ɛgzm̩ | SSB. 'eggs and (bacon)' |
| 'ɬʊkŋ̍ | Nor. 'looking' |
| juɣŋ̍ | SSB. 'you can' |

*Other liquids (syllabic 'r', 'w')*

There is little evidence for a phonetic sequence [əɹ] within word boundaries in varieties of English in which /r/ is an approximant (Scots English is an exception, though the reflexes of /r/ are not always approximants). Unstressed syllables spelled 'ar', 'er', 'ir', 'or', or 'ur' are pronounced [ɚ] in American English and are represented by some other form of central vowel in most British varieties. But [ə] + [ɹ] sequences *can* occur across word boundaries, as in:

| | |
|---|---|
| ɚd'ɹəʊz | 'a red rose' |
| 'dʒæfɚeɪzɨnz | 'Jaffa raisins' |
| ɹɪ'mɛmbɹ̩ | Psmsh. 'remember her' |

and these are realized as [ɚ] in many accents: r-colouring is simply superimposed on the schwa. This could be regarded as the creation of a syllabic 'r' by the same process, as reflected in Lodge's transcription for Peasmarsh, above.

It is not commonly noted that it is possible to achieve something which might be called a 'syllabic w' in some cases (but see Ogden, 1999: 73 for similar cases). For example, in SSB. when you say 'The dogs were barking', what is spelled 'were' can be pronounced as a rounded schwa that might also be described as a syllabic w. One might say again that the vowel and consonant gestures overlap completely and that the resulting segment does the work of both. Here, however, the schwa notionally follows the resonant rather than preceding it as it did in the cases above.

Other examples:

| | |
|---|---|
| ðeɪwz | Psmsh. 'they was' |
| wz̥ | Ed. 'was (actually)' |
| wz | Nor. 'was' |
| sɛdwjʊu | Psmsh. 'said, well you . . .' |
| wɪtʃəz | Am. 'which was' |
| ə'bɪʊdɪŋ | SSB. 'were building' |

### Fricatives

Obstruents can also be syllabic if they have enough energy to function as a syllable nucleus. The most obvious candidates are fricatives, and there are many cases where a fricative in an unstressed syllable can function as a syllable. Many cases are underlying 's' + schwa + voiceless obstruent sequences, like 'suspicion', 'support' and 'satanic.' [ʃ] can show the same feature in sequences like

'Shapiro' [ʃˈpɪɹəʊ] or 'hit you' [ˈhɪtʃ]. Less common is syllabic 'f' 'for pity's sake' [fˈpɪtɪ], or 'if Tom's there' [f̩ ˈtɒmzɛə].

Syllabic fricatives are usually formed by the overlap with a following schwa rather than a preceding one, in contrast with most examples above. Other examples:

| | |
|---|---|
| ʃbˈweɪs̩t | ShB. 'should waste' |
| äʃtθɪŋk | Psmsh. 'I should think' |
| ð ˈdosbemˈmɛn | Stkpt. 'the dustbinmen' |
| β̃ | Stkpt. 'I'm (not)' |
| ˈætʃ | Am. 'that you' |
| ˈmækṣməm | Am. 'maximum' |
| fgaʔ | ELon. 'forgot' (Wells, 1982: 321) |

It would be possible to contend that what is happening in the case of voiceless syllabic fricatives is schwa devoicing. While this is a very reasonable abstract explanation, there is often no phonetic evidence of a separate segment resembling a voiceless vowel: the fricative quality is consistent throughout. Lodge, however, offers the following examples, in which he transcribes a voiceless vowel:

| | |
|---|---|
| ˈbʋetẹʃ | Stkpt. 'British (Home Stores)' |
| eʔ kaʃẹ | Stkpt. 'it costs you (twenty . . . )' |
| ˈafə̥tʰn | Stkpt. 'Offerton' |

One might initially imagine that sequences such as 'support' and 'sport' could become homonymous thorough this process, but in addition to having a longer (and perhaps even louder) 's', the 'p' of the former can retain aspiration, thus showing its syllable-initial status. In the (much less frequent) case of this process occurring before a liquid (as in 'if Ray's there' [fˈɹeɪzɛə]), the liquid does not normally devoice, again maintaining its syllable-initial identity. (But see Fokes and Bond, 1993.)

## Voiceless vowels

It is sometimes claimed that voiceless stops are syllabic in sequences such as 'potato' [pʰˈtɛɪtəʊ]. While one might see the parallel with syllabic fricatives, I feel inclined to reject this analysis, since voiceless stops in themselves have so little energy. (The Lancashire/Yorkshire [d:oɹ] for 'the door' might be considered a counterexample, but the term 'syllabic plosive' still seems anomalous. Perhaps one could invoke the notion of mora instead of syllable in this case.)

Aspiration is not normally expected in unstressed syllables, so claiming that the aspiration of the stop is the syllabic bit also seems questionable. In sequences like these (which can even appear across word boundaries as in 'to play' [tʰ'pl̥eɪ]), what appears to be aspiration can much more reasonably be analysed as a voiceless vowel, as suggested in Rodgers (1999).

Other examples:

| | | |
|---|---|---|
| pʰ'ɫsmən | Psmsh. | 'policemen' |
| tʰ'go | Am. | 'to go' |
| kʰd̥ | Am. | 'could' |
| pʰ'tɪkəli | Am. | 'particularly' |

$$\left[ p ə l i s \right] \; vs$$
$$\left[ p ə̥ l i s \right]$$

There are, of course, cases where syllables are lost: 'medicine', 'camera', and many other words are sometimes said with two syllables though they indubitably began with three. Yet I would contend that English tends to preserve the suprasegmental properties of utterances – stress, duration, intonation – even where there is some 'slippage' in the linear nature of the segmental structure. One might imagine, along with Browman and Goldstein (1992), that the schwa and resonant are completely overlapping in the syllabic resonants, so that the articulatory qualities of the resonant and the syllabic properties of the vowel are preserved (though Kohler (1992) makes a convincing argument that this explanation cannot always hold for German).

### Schwa suppression (vowel coalescence)

A process which goes against the generalization suggested above, reducing the number of syllables by one, is incorporation of a schwa into a neighbouring vowel of a more peripheral nature. The schwa is assimilated by the neighbouring vowel, so that perceived syllabicity is not preserved. Sometimes the remaining vowel seems longer than it would otherwise.

| | | |
|---|---|---|
| gəʊ'wɛɪ | SSB. 'go away' | *VV* → *V* |
| tɹaɪ'gɛn | SSB. 'try again' | |
| ði'kæɾəmi | Am. 'the academy' | |
| gɐː | Am. 'got a' | |
| tʰoðə | Stkpt. 'the other' | |
| tʰæv | ShB. 'to have' | |
| tʰæv | Psmsh. 'to have' | |
| biŋ | Ed. 'being' | |
| 'ðʊðə | Cov. 'the other' | |
| ɛ̃tsəbæo | Am. 'and it's about' | |

(Wells 1982: 216) discusses a similar process with SSB. centring diphthongs [skɛːs], [fɔːs] for [skɛəs] 'scarce' and [fɔəs] 'force', also yielding [faː] for 'fire' and [tɑː] for 'tower'. He calls this 'Monophthongization'. He also observes (p. 434) that in Irish, schwa can disappear after a vowel and before a liquid or nasal, with the corresponding loss of a syllable. 'Lion', for example, can be pronounced [laɪn] and 'seeing' as [siːn]. These appear to be restricted versions of the schwa suppression presented above.

### 2.3.2  Reduction of closure for obstruents

We have mentioned that completely unstressed vowels in English seem targetless: their quality is determined by their environment. The situation for obstruents is less drastic: targets seen to exist, but are not always fully achieved in unstressed syllables (Turk (1992: 124) shows, for example, that all stops are relatively short in an unstressed position). The result examined here is that consonants can be more open than might be expected in their traditional descriptions: stops lose their closure and fricatives can show barely enough approximation to allow for turbulence (see EPG displays in chapter 4). Lenition or weakening is especially marked in syllables immediately following a stressed syllable which no doubt plays a part in creating a contrast.

Voiceless stops do not normally become recognizable fricatives, largely due to lack of sufficient airflow (cf. Shockey and Gibbon, 1993). They are most easily recognized through the lack of a perceptible release. In addition, unclosed, 't' and 'd' do not resemble 's' and 'z' because the tongue position is coronal for the former and laminal for the latter. Brown (1996) uses a retroflex symbol ([ʂ, ʐ]) for incompletely closed alveolar stops to express this difference. Incompletely closed voiced stops can resemble voiced fricatives very closely, but open /d/ is not [ð] because it is alveolar, not dental.

| | |
|---|---|
| 'peɪɸo | Stkpt. 'people' |
| ɐ'ɣo | Stkpt. 'I go' |
| pʋe'sɛnd | Stkpt. 'pretend' |
| pɪɸö | ShB. 'people' |
| əβæʋʔ | Psmsh. 'about' |
| əβɪ | Psmsh. 'to be' |
| ɹeçəgnæɪz | Ed. 'recognize' |
| jüss'ɔwɨẓ | Ed. 'used to always' |
| 'bɛːçən | Nor. 'bacon' |
| km'plɪʂɪd | Brown, SSB. 'completed' |
| juɣŋ | SSB. 'you can' |
| bɨɣɔz | SSB. 'because' |
| ĩvæɯʔju | SSB. 'in fact you' |
| 'fɹaɪd̥ɪ | SSB. 'Friday' |
| wĩɲɪɣo | Am. 'when you go' |
| ɛɪxip | Am. 'they keep' |
| 'ʧʌxəʔ | Nor. 'chuck it' |
| əβaʋʔ | Cov. 'about' |
| ɳɪt̬gɐt | Am. 'and it got' |
| ɔ'ɹɛz̥ɪ | Brown, SSB. 'already' |

Relaxed speech generally displays less contact for consonants than careful speech when viewed using an electropalate (Hardcastle, personal communication; Shockey, 1991; Shockey and Farnetani, 1992), and unstressed syllables generally show more articulatory undershoot than stressed ones, so the reductions discussed in this section can be seen to have a strong phonetic component. On the other hand, processes such as these must be a source of phonological lenition.

### 2.3.3   *Tapping*

This is called 'flapping' by most phonologists, but the flap is a retroflex tap and the sounds to be discussed here are not remotely retroflex.

Tapping in English is a process whereby an alveolar stop or cluster is pronounced in a ballistic rather than in a controlled fashion. Sounds like [t, d, n, nt] are characterized by closing and opening phases which are precisely controlled. The tap [ɾ] is produced by a single gesture of 'throwing' the tongue towards the alveolar ridge, then letting it drop back. A tap normally is achieved in 30–40 msec., which makes it the fastest consonant (barring the individual cycles of a trill) (Lehiste, 1970: 13). Normally, the tap is a voiced sound, though a voiceless one is certainly possible to achieve. Fox and Terbeek (1977) found in an Am. corpus that 19 per cent of taps were voiceless.

Tapping is a strong feature of American, Australian and Irish English. Some linguists regard it as obligatory for most American accents under normal conditions when there is a /t/ or /d/ preceded by a stressed vowel and followed by an unstressed vowel. (This environment seems conducive to lenition in general: weakening of closure is often found here as well for non-alveolar obstruents and for /t, d/ in SSB.) American speakers can, of course, evince a perfectly acceptable intervocalic [t] or [d] in very slow or extra-careful speech or when metrically challenged, as in:

> Oh, there was a good ship and she sailed upon the sea;
> And the name of that ship, it was the Golden VaniTy . . .

In fact, the conditions for tapping are not yet fully understood (though see Zue and Laferriere, 1979 and de Jong, 1998). Vaux (2000) proposes the following conditions for General American: 'flapping' applies to alveolar stops (a) after a sonorant other than l, m, or ŋ, but with restrictions on n; (b) before an unstressed vowel within words or before any vowel across a word boundary; (c) when

not in foot-initial position. It is commonly thought not to occur at
the beginning of stressed syllables, but appears in American expres-
sions such as 'Get out of here' [gɪɾˈaɾəɦɪɹ] (Beckman, personal communication) and has been observed in the Australian pronunciation
of words such as 'eighteen'.

For Am., tapping is indubitably a feature of even careful speech
and is therefore not particular to conversational speech. In Australian, Cockney, and Irish it is, in contrast, more restricted: it applies
only to underlying /t/ and occurs only sporadically rather than
unexceptionally.

Tapping is a much less prominent feature of SSB., but many
speakers employ it for /t/ occasionally, especially in often-heard
words such as 'British' and (in a linguistics context) 'phonetics'. SSB.
speakers more frequently choose the option of incomplete closure
in the tapping environment, but tapping remains an option for many
British accents. Scottish English does not include this process, possibly because the tap is a frequent realization of Scottish /r/. Some
Midlands accents (e.g. Coventry) do, however, show both tapping
and a tapped realization of /r/, so they are not mutually exclusive.

| | |
|---|---|
| ˈgɒɾˈɪn | ShB. 'got in' |
| ˈlɪvɪnɪɾˈʌp | ShB. 'living it up' |
| ˈɛnɪbaɾɪ | Psmsh. 'anybody' |
| baɾm̩ | Psmsh. 'bottom' |
| ˈbɛɾɪʒ | Cov. 'bet his (geraniums)' |
| ˈgɛɾin | Cov. 'getting' |
| pʊɾəp | SSB. 'put up' |
| wʌɾɛvə | SSB. 'whatever' |
| sɔɾəv | SSB. 'sort of' |
| pəɾɐɪ | SSB. 'but I' |

### 2.3.4   Devoicing and voicing

Impressionistically speaking, speakers of English avoid voicing in
obstruents when possible. Phonologically voiced stops are rarely
voiced phonetically, and when they are, they are very rarely fully
voiced. Voiced fricatives fare a bit better, but /z/ is hardly ever
fully voiced. It has often been observed that voicing is made difficult

P (voice) measures

during obstruents by the pressure which develops behind the obstruction: the difference between subglottal and supraglottal pressure falls, and extra effort is needed to maintain vibration. Speakers of many languages (Greek, most of the Romance languages) find ways of overcoming the inconvenience, but English speakers seem to resort, instead, to alternative methods for signalling voicing (aspiration or lack of it, preceding vowel length). Thus one sees in English a reflection of the universal tendency for languages to have voiceless obstruents as the unmarked case (see chapter 4).

| | |
|---|---|
| ʋeˈleɪʋ̥ | Stkpt. 'relieve (people)' |
| ʃɛɬʋz̥ | Stkpt. 'shelves' (sentence-final) |
| ðɹiz̥ | ShB. 'these (people)' |
| wɵz̥ | Psmsh. 'was (called)' |
| kɔːɬd̥ | Psmsh. 'called (something)' |
| ɪz̥ | Psmsh. 'is (nearest)' |
| ˈbæʃfəɹdz̥ | Psmsh. 'bashfords (lived)' |
| ˈkoɬigz̥ | Ed. 'colleagues (in)' |
| dæʊnˈstɛːz̥ | Cov. 'downstairs' (utterance-final) |
| ˈwɵz̥ | Nor. 'was' (utterance-final) |
| jɑɹts | Am. 'yards (w)' |
| jəʋ̥ | Am. 'you've (g)' |
| stæts | Am. 'stands (n)' |
| hjʉʧ | SSB. 'huge (tatty)' |
| ænd̥ʰ | SSB. 'and (Rusty)' |
| wəz̥ | Ed. 'was (the)' |
| ʧɛʊd̥ | Ed. 'child (you)' |
| nəz̥ ˈtʊu | Cov. 'there's two' |
| pkɔz | Brown, SSB. 'because' |
| ˈlɛʔəz̥ | Nor. 'letters (right)' |

While some of this devoicing may be conditioned by the following voiceless consonant, you will observe that many cases are followed by voicing. — not in the list above!

Conversely, in conversational speech one occasionally finds voiced segments where one expects to find voiceless ones. A principal environment in which this occurs is the same as the one which most often conditions tapping (roughly between a stressed and an unstressed vowel), and of course the tap is also normally voiced. 'Voicing through' can, however, occur more generally intervocalically in relatively unstressed position. It is especially likely to occur in continuant consonants and can often be found in syllables where stops have become continuant.

These might be called cases of 'double lenition': reduction of closure and voicing of voiceless segments are both seen seen as weakening or lenition, as in Verner's Law: 'voiceless stops go to voiced fricatives when enclosed by voiced sounds and preceded by an unaccented vowel.'

| | |
|---|---|
| pɾɒdɨstənt | Ed. 'protestant' |
| bədaɪ'θīɣɪn | SSB. 'But I think in . . .' |
| 'gɑdə | Cov. 'got a' |
| 'tʊgid | Cov. 'took it (out)' |
| 'pɑdɨgət | Nor. 'Pottergate' |

## 2.4   Syllabic Conditioning Factors

### 2.4.1   *Syllable shape*

English is known to be a language with a potential for very heavy syllables when compared with most other languages of the world. A CCCVCCC syllable is not unusual in English ('scrimped, splints').

A database of syllable structures (Fudge and Shockey, 1998) reflects the following distribution in about 200 randomly-chosen languages:

Loosy presentation

28 or 15 per cent of languages allow syllable-initial three-consonant clusters.
86 or 45 per cent of languages allow initial two-consonant clusters.
7 or 4 per cent of languages allow final three-consonant clusters.
18 or 9 per cent of languages allow final two-consonant clusters.
131 or 69 per cent have an obligatory syllable-initial consonant.
None has an obligatory null onset.
15 or 8 per cent have an obligatory syllable-final consonant.
23 or 12 per cent have an obligatory null coda.

These results support the commonly-held opinion that the unmarked syllable in languages of the world has one initial consonant and at most one final consonant. In spontaneous speech, English moves toward the mean by reducing the number of adjacent consonants: 'a regular alternation of consonants and vowels is more natural than clusterings' (Wells, 1982: 96).

While it is not always possible to arrive at the closed-open (CV) pattern, several processes, outlined below, work together to minimize sequences of either consonants or vowels. This may be another example of the 'phonological conspiracy' postulated by Kisseberth (1970).

### 2.4.2   *Onsets and codas*

There is an enormous difference in type and frequency of connected speech processes at the beginnings versus the ends of syllables: syllable onsets are much more resistant to change than codas. The relative weakness of syllable-final consonants could be said to be reflected in their distribution: in most languages, the syllable-final inventory is considerably smaller than the initial one, generally having a subset relation. Deletion of final consonants is heavily documented both diachronically and synchronically in the phonologies of the world's languages (French being a very striking case), whereas deletion of initial consonants is unusual. Dalby (1984) stresses the importance of this distinction in English casual speech processes.

In English, the type of cluster allowed is, of course, different initially and finally: barring clusters beginning with /s/, sonority increases in word-initial clusters and decreases in word-final ones. The fact that final clusters are not identical to initial ones is a partial explanation for why the two sets undergo different reduction processes.

Alternatively, in an information theory framework, one might claim that codas are more redundant than onsets and therefore carry a smaller functional load: once the onset and nucleus are in place, the number of possibilities for completing the syllable, given existing vocabulary, are diminished (but still large in many cases in English).

Stress also plays an important part. In general, onsets of stressed syllables are resistant to change, onsets of syllables which do not immediately follow a stressed syllable are fairly stable, and onsets of syllables immediately following a stressed syllable are vulnerable, especially if they are a single plosive (not part of a cluster), even more if they are alveolar plosive.

Three different phonological processes are very common in this post-stress environment: (1) tapping, (2) voicing through and (3) reduction of closure, as mentioned above.

### 2.4.3   CVCV *alternation*

Reduction shrinks consonant clusters: some phonological processes of English reduce the adjacency of vowels, hence discouraging VV sequences.

#### Careful speech

We can see two instances in the phonology of careful speech where English shows a tendency to prefer alternating consonants and vowels rather than two vowels in a row: one is the well-known a/an alternation, the other is the process in SSB. where a linking r is inserted between a non-high word-final vowel and a following word-initial vowel, as in 'Anna and the King of Siam' ['ænəɹən . . . ]. One might even claim that the well-known [ðə/ði] alternation (the car, the apple) creates an approximant-like gesture in the second case which contributes to a CVCV-like articulation: [ðij'æpɬ]. Whether or not a true consonant is introduced, this process creates the same kind of close-open gesture with which one defines a simple syllable.

#### Spontaneous speech

Two connected speech processes which contribute to preserving a CV-type, syllable structure are (1) the [v/0] alternation in the word 'of' and (2) the loss of tongue contact for /l/ syllable-finally. The former of these is well-known and well-documented, and in fact, 'of' is frequently cited as a word which has a 'weak form' (Cruttenden, 2001: 253). While it is always possible to pronounce the word 'of' as [əv] or even [ɑv], it is typically reduced to [ə] when followed by a consonant: 'lots of apples', [lɒtsəv'æpḷz] but 'lots of jobs' [lɒtsə'dʒɒbz].

The 'weak and strong forms' of 'of' are much more like the 'a/an' forms of the indefinite article in English, the main difference being that it is not actually unheard of to say 'lots [əv] cars' whereas it is wrong (or, at best, eccentric) to say 'let's take an bus.'

Word-final [v] is occasionally omitted in other cases, most notice-ably before another fricative ('I don't belieVE that', 'four, fiVE, six', 'leaVEs in the gutter'). This seems idiosyncratic and may be most common in Am., though Brown gives examples from SSB. (1996: 68).

The second is sometimes called 'l-vocalization' the notion being that as dark (velarized) /l/ loses the tongue-tip contact with the alveolar ridge (as it can before a consonant or pause), it becomes more like a vowel, hence decreasing the number of articulated consonant clusters. While it is claimed that there is a spectrum of different realizations of syllable-final /l/ in some accents of English so that 'l' vocalizes gradually (Hardcastle and Barry, 1985; Wright, 1989: 358; Kerswill, 1995: 197), my work in Am. and SSB. sug-gests that there is an underlying binary pattern: contact suggests the presence of a consonant while none suggests the presence of a vowel. The resolution of this difference of opinion lies in deciding how much tongue-palate contact can be allowed for a vowel and what it means for a consonant to be 'partially vocalized'. Bauer (1986: 231) reports that in New Zealand English, vocalized /l/ is so prevalent that many people cannot make a dark [l] preconsonantally, so that hypercorrect light [l] is sometimes heard in words such as 'milk'. These data suggest that we are moving towards a *phonetic* CVCV structure. (It is not being argued that the /l/ is actually absent phonologically: the heavily velarized vowel which remains can only be interpreted as representing a phonological /l/.)

| ɔ:wɪz | ShB. 'always' |
| fɔ:ö | ShB. 'fall' (that) |
| əʒ 'juuʒʊ | Psmsh. 'as usual' |
| dɹədfö | Psmsh. 'dreadful' |
| skuö | Ed. 'school' |

| | |
|---|---|
| 'odə̥r | Ed. 'older' |
| ɔːɹɔɪp | Cov. 'all right' |
| izsɛö̥ | Cov. 'hisself' |
| wɐːz̥ | Am. 'walls' |
| 'pipotş | Am. 'people that's' |
| 'bɪwɾə | Am. 'built a' |
| 'pipɤ | SSB. 'people' |
| 'əʊd'mɪl | Brown, SSB. 'old mill' |
| 'kʌmɪneɪtɪd | Brown, SSB. 'culminated' |

### 2.4.4   Syllable-final adjustments

Cluster simplification is very common in connected speech. But it is not just any cluster which is likely to have surface form very different from citation form: the word 'jumps' for example, has a cluster which seems very similar to the one in 'hunts', yet the latter is far more likely to reduce. Further, if followed by the word 'frequently', the probability of the final cluster reducing in the former is not significantly raised, while the final cluster in the latter becomes ever more vulnerable. There is an interaction of factors: syllable-final, before another consonant cluster, and alveolar all play their part.

We have mentioned above that syllable-final /l/ is likely to lose its oral contact when followed by a consonant, at least in those varieties of English where final /l/ is velarized. The same can be said for /l/ in a word-internal cluster. Loss of contact is somewhat less likely to occur across word boundaries when the following sound is phonetically alveolar, and the same can be said for the syllable-internal case: it will occur more in words such as 'shelf' and 'milk' than in 'salt' and 'halls' in accents where there is variability in its occurrence.

### Alteration of final /t/ and /d/

Word- or syllable-final /t/ is very prone to change. Other than the tapping and lenition mentioned above, its most common fate is to be realized as either a glottal stop or a [t] which is fully coarticulated with a glottal stop. The latter is termed 'glottal reinforcement' (Wells, 1982: 260) and can occur wherever the full glottal stop is found. Obviously, the only difference between a glottal stop and a glottally-reinforced [t̰ʔ] is that the tip of the tongue makes contact with the alveolar ridge in the latter case but not in the former. Holmes (1994: 441) remarks that hearing the difference between a glottally-reinforced [t̰ʔ] and a glottal stop in a preconsonantal environment is very difficult and that the use of spectrograms to distinguish the two is not especially helpful.

In many American and British English accents, final voiceless stops which occur before a consonant or silence have a tendency to be glottally reinforced, but it is only /t/ which loses its oral gesture. (Fibreoptic endoscopy has shown that initial voiceless stops in stressed syllables in English are articulated with an open glottis, so we must conclude that phonological voicelessness can be reflected in more than one laryngeal gesture.)

| | |
|---|---|
| ɐgaʔˈgʊɐed | Stkpt. 'I got Grade' |
| æˈɛeteʔ | Stkpt. 'I hate it' |
| boʔðeˈsɛz | Stkpt. '. . . but they says' |
| ˈðæʔˈweɪ | ShB. 'that way' |
| ˈpɛɪnʔpɒt | ShB. 'paintpot' |
| ˈpeɪvmɨnʔ | Psmsh. 'pavement' |
| əβæoʔ | Psmsh. 'about (midnight)' |
| kwʌɪʔ | Ed. 'quite (near)' |
| dʌʊmʔ | Cov. 'don't (bother)' |
| ˈaüʔsaɪd | Nor 'outside' |
| ˈdʌzə̄ʔˈwʌ̄ʔ | SSB. 'doesn't want' |
| ˈkwaɪʔgʊd | SSB. 'quite good' |
| ˈgrɛɪʔbɪg | Am. 'great big' |
| gɪʔˈbɔɹd | Am. 'get bored' |
| spɛ̄ʔ | Am. 'spent' |
| wɔzn̩ʔ | Ed. 'wasn't' |
| nɔʔ | Ed. 'not (nowadays)' |
| ɫaɪʔˈðæʔ | Nor. 'like that' |
| ɛːʔn̩ | Cov. 'out on' |

Cockney (originally East-Central London) can substitute glottal stop for final /p/ and /k/ (making 'clot, clop, and clock' homonymous) and, in common with Lodge's (1984) Norwich and Edinburgh accents, can substitute glottal stop for /t/ intervocalically. While not central to the arguments put forth here, this does confirm that the tendency to glottal replacement is stronger in some accents. Wells (p. 592) reports (in 1982) that there is little or no t-glottalling in Southern Hemisphere English, but Holmes, writing in 1994, contends that glottally-reinforced [t] and glottal stop are increasingly common in New Zealand. She notes, on the other hand, that of more than 3,000 cases of intervocalic /t/ in her database, none was articulated as glottal stop (p. 461).

In Am. and SSB., t > ʔ is especially common before labials, so that 'hot water' and 'hatband' are highly likely to be articulated with glottal stop, whereas 'hotcakes' and 'Kitkat' are sometimes not.

Pronunciation of /t/ as glottal stop rarely happens when the /t/ ends a consonant cluster, but when closure is lost for a (notionally) preceding consonant, the glottal stop can appear. One frequently hears, for example, the pronunciation [kãʔ] for 'can't' (see 'nasal relocation' below). When /t/ appears after a /l/, it can become a glottal stop if the lateral is pronounced without dorsal contact ('vocalized'), e.g. [sɔ:ʔ] for 'salt'.

/t/ can disappear when preceded and followed by consonants, especially when followed by a labial. 'Last place' and 'first one' rarely show a [t] with complete closure in spontaneous speech. When /t/ is followed by /t/ or /d/ as in 'last time' or 'last dime' it is difficult to say whether it has any articulatory correlates, but often one can detect no voiceless stop in other sequences involving 's': 'last night', 'last light', 'first season'. The latter example, involving an [sts] cluster, is one in which a fully articulated [t] is virtually never found, but often with compensation in the length of the fricative: ['pəʊs:ɛʃn̩l 'tɛs:] 'postsessional tests'.

We see historical evidence of this process in words such as 'Christmas', 'hasten', 'castle', where the option to pronounce the spelled 't' is no longer available.

/t/ is very likely to be pronounced when preceded by another consonant and followed by a dental fricative, and in 'didn't think', 'passed that', 'left this'. It is possible that the perceived [t] is a passing or epenthetic segment like the phantom [p] in 'hamster': certainly in my own speech it is possible to hear an unexpected [t] in 'one thing' [wəntθɪŋ].

Fabricius (2000) suggests that for SSB. t-glottalling before consonants is ubiquitous and regarded as normal, t-glottalling utterance-
finally is common but still regarded as a casual rather than a formal
feature, and intervocalic t-glottalling is both regarded as informal
and restricted to the London area.

| | |
|---|---|
| 'weɪkes | Stkpt. 'weakest (little)' |
| 'ʤʌs | ShB. 'just (the)' |
| 'ɹisbɔːn | ShB. 'Eastbourne' |
| 'ɔɹgənɪss | Psmsh. 'organist (from)' |
| 'feɹˌslaɪn | Psmsh. 'first line' |
| dɪdn̩ | Psmsh. 'didn't' |
| 'issæɪd | Ed. 'east side' |
| 'ɫaːʃɪə | Cov. 'last year' |
| ɪz | Cov. 'it's' |
| 'bɪgɪs paːt | Cov. 'biggest part' |
| 'bɹɔgkɑːsːə'njus | SSB. 'broadcast the news' |
| 'æspɛks | Brown, SSB. 'aspects' |
| dɪdn̩ | Psmsh. 'didn't' |
| ɹɪ'spɛkfɚ | Am. 'respect for' |
| fʌɹsθɹi | Ed. 'first three' |
| 'donno | Ed. 'don't know' |
| 'dɪstɹɨks | Ed. 'districts' |
| ɹʌfəs'pʰɫɛːs | Nor. 'roughest place' |
| 'fəsʤab | Cov. 'first job' |
| 'kɛpɪt | Cov. 'kept it' |

Final /d/ also may have no phonetic correlates when sandwiched between two consonants, as in 'They closed my account' ['klozmaɪ . . . ]
or 'misjudged completely' [mɪs'ʤʌʧkəm . . . ].

/d/ is frequently not perceptibly produced after /n/, as in 'Hand
me a nut' ['hænmi] or ['hæmːi]. This can happen even before silence
in Am.: '(marching) band' [bæn]. Even if the /l/ is pronounced
without tongue contact, the absence of phonetic [d] is possible in
final 'ld' clusters when followed by another consonant: hold me
['houmi], boldface ['boufəɪs]. Most Americans with a proofreading
bent can report having seen the hypercorrect 'cold slaw' on a menu
at least once.

| | |
|---|---|
| ən'eɪ | Stkpt. 'and he' |
| 'fæʊnnɛm | Stkpt. 'found them' |
| ɹaʊn: | ShB. 'round' |
| ʌʊɫ'mæn | Psmsh. 'old man' |
| n̩'frɛnz̥ | Ed. 'and friends' |
| 'tʌʊɫmi | Cov. 'told me' |
| 'kʰʌʊɫ'nɪp | Nor. 'cold nip' |
| sə'spɛndɪfɹəm | Brown, SSB. 'suspended from' |
| 'bæɱfə'laɪf | Brown, SSB. 'banned for life' |

There is no tendency for glottal reinforcement of final /d/ (even when unvoiced) except in cases where it is conventionally pronounced as [t], as in some people's rendition of 'had to' ['hæʔtə].

## Nasal relocation

When one finds a phonological final sequence VNC (especially where the final consonant is a voiceless stop), it is very common for the phonetic reflex to be 'nasalized vowel + consonant'. Normally we expect the underlying NC cluster to be homorganic, and the process is especially common in English for final -nt clusters (cf. Wells, 1982: 317).

This could be seen as a re-timing of velum lowering and oral closure: nasalization begins earlier than one might expect from the citation shape, and articulator contact is later.

```
Citation form V   |-----------|
             N               |-----------|
             C                           |-------|
Relaxed form V   |---------------|
             N   |-------------|
             C                 |------|
```

Examples:

| | |
|---|---|
| tʰɸ̃:z | Stkpt. 'turns' |
| dõʊ̃ʔ | Stkpt. 'don't' |

| | |
|---|---|
| ə̃ | Stkpt. 'and' |
| aθĩʔ | ShB. 'I think' |
| wɛw̃wɪ | ShB. 'when we' |
| wɛw̃wɪ | Psmsh. 'when we' |
| tɹɑːz̃pɔ·ʔ | Psmsh. 'transport' |
| 'ɛniθĩg | Cov. 'anything' |
| 'fɔɪvstʌũw | Cov. 'fivestones (when)' |
| dʌzə̃ʔ'wã̃ʔ | SSB. 'doesn't want' |
| 'sʌ̃θɪŋ | SSB. 'something' |
| ə̃ɐ'θĩmɐɪ | SSB. 'and I think my' |
| kɨnvĩst | Am. 'convinced' |
| kæp | Am. 'camp' |
| ə̃'ləs | Am. 'unless' |
| əz̃ʃi | Cov. 'and she' |
| 'ɛĩʔ | Cov. 'ain't' |
| ĩðə'fɔm | Brown, SSB. 'in the form' |

It is possible that the percept of a nasal consonant is produced 'cost free': as the velum closes for the consonant, it passes the threshold of closure which is required to give a momentary impression of a nasal segment. This would allow there to be a discrepancy between the number of articulatory gestures produced (two: raise velum and move tongue) and the number of perceived segments (three: nasal vowel, nasal, consonant).

```
Relaxed form? V   |---------------|
                C          |------|
```

Whatever model is most likely, the process described above can lead to a phonetic distinction between plain versus nasalized vowels in pairs such as cap/camp and cart/can't (SSB.) cat/can't (Am.). Cohn (1993) argues for this being a phonetic rather than a phonological process in English. There is little evidence that the process can apply to a simple VC sequence, though, of course, the effect can be evinced across word boundaries in sequences like 'one, two, three'.

As mentioned briefly in chapter 5, vowel nasalization before a nasal consonant and loss of the habit of making the closure for the nasal is thought to be the source of the phonemically nasal vowels of French (e.g. beau/bon) and Portuguese (se/sim [si/sĩ]) where it is said to be 'phonologized' because the distinction has formally passed from the consonant to the vowel. Clearly, English can not be said to have gone that far phonologically.

It is striking that, at least in English, this process does not seem to occur before voiced stops: words like 'band, around' are much more likely to be realized without the final [d] (in final position or before another consonant) than without the nasal segment. The voiced alveolar sequences thus follow the pattern of the labial and velar 'bomb', 'limb', 'tomb', 'sing' sequences in most accents in non-pronunciation of the final stop, though they are not yet standard pronunciation.

### 2.4.5   Syllable shape again

Below is the citation form of a sentence collected from one of my Am. speakers ('And the scientists are always saying that there's no life on Mars'), followed by the actual realization:

> ænddə'saɪəntɨstsɑɹɔlwɪz'sɛɪɨŋðætðɛɹznoɯ'laɪfɑnmɑɹz
> VCCCVVCCVCCCVCVCCVCCVCVC CVCCVC CVCC

> nə'saɪnəsɹɔɪ'sɛɪnəttɛɹsnoɯ'laɪfɑmɑɹz
> CVCVCVCCVCVCV CVCCCV CVCVCVCC

In the former, there are eight consonant clusters, six of two consonants and two of three consonants. In the latter, we see three consonant clusters, two of two consonants and one of three. The movement towards a CVCV structure is clear, though not complete.

## 2.5   Other Processes

These can be roughly described as processes which operate at the beginnings of words and which primarily affect short, closed-class words.

## 2.5.1  *ð-reduction*

This is the process whereby initial [ð] in words such as 'the, this, that' becomes assimilated to a previous alveolar consonant (cf. Lodge, 1984; Manuel, 1995). Several different phonetic realizations are possible, ranging from moving the tongue forward from alveolar to dental while maintaining the other characteristics of the alveolar consonant:

what the heck   wɒtd̪ə'ɦɛk
run the mile   ɹənn̪ə'maɪɤ

> Voicing assimilation is possible:   wɒtt̪ə'ɦɛk
> as well as manner assimilation:   fɹəmn̪ə 'from the'
> and complete assimilation:   ɹən:ə'maɪɤ

The retained alveolar (e.g. the [n] in 'run') is normally longer than usual, suggesting a compensation for the lost (or severely under-articulated) dental fricative. The lengthened consonant can thus be the only cue to distinguish the definite and indefinite articles (e.g. 'run the mile/run a mile'). An experiment which I did some time ago (Shockey, 1978) confirmed that listeners can use consonant length as a perceptual cue for underlying Consonant + [ð] collocations in these cases. In some cases, there is no extra length, a process referred to by phonologists as 'degemination'.

'aɬə't^ha:m   Stkpt. 'all the time'
'senəməzzɛ:   Stkpt. 'cinemas there'
watʃenn̪ə   Stkpt. 'watching the'
ənn̪æʔs   ShB. 'and that's'
wɒzzɛm   ShB. 'was them'
'ɔ:ɬ'lɪs   ShB. 'all this'
kɔ:ɬɬəm   Psmsh. 'call them'
bɪ'twɪinn̪ə   Psmsh. 'between the'
ən'n̪aʕ   Ed. 'and that (was)'
'tekssəm   Ed. 'takes them'
inn̪ə   Cov. 'in the'
ɪnn̪iz   SSB. 'in these'

| | |
|---|---|
| ɛ̃ŋɛɹ | SSB. 'And they're' |
| ɔːʈis | SSB. 'All these' |
| 'wɛntə' | Brown, SSB. 'went the' |
| æoʈɛɹ | Am. 'out there' |
| wɚdət | Am. 'word that' |
| 'kɔɹsːɛɪ | Am. 'course they' |
| 'wəŋ̃ŋi | Nor. 'when the' |
| əŋ̃ŋə | Nor. 'and the' |
| izˈzaʔ | Cov. 'is that' |
| ä̤ɬɬəz | Cov. 'well, there's' |

## 2.5.2   *h-dropping*

This is a process which varies considerably from accent to accent of English Most of the accents represented here show reduction of /h/ when it is in a short, unstressed word (usually a pronoun or an auxiliary verb), especially when preceded by another fricative (but see Al-Tamimi (2002) for evidence that h-loss is not conditioned by a previous fricative in SSB. or Cockney). It is common to hear 'What does he [dəzi] want' and 'She'll have [əv] gone by now.' The Stockport accent, on the other hand, appears not to use [h] at all, and Peasmarsh only in the occasional focal noun.

For accents which characteristically realize /h/ fully at the beginning of stressed syllables, loss in unstressed positions normally happens after a consonant: between vowels, /h/ becomes voiced but does not typically get lost completely. This reflects comments on syllable shape as seen above.

This is a casual speech process which has been covered relatively well (for prestigious accents) by the standard texts on English pronunciation, so it needn't be pursued further here (but see the comments below on 'weak forms').

## 2.5.3   *'Palatalization'*

This somewhat misnamed process is the one whereby either (1) an underlying alveolar fricative followed by a /j/ becomes postalveolar or (2) an underlying /j/ preceded by an alveolar stop becomes a postalveolar fricative. This process is largely conditioned by words such as 'you', 'your', 'yet' and by a few other common words such as 'year' and 'usual' as seen below.

Within a word, these pronunciations have become conventional.

| | | | |
|---|---|---|---|
| press + ure | pressure | please + ure | pleasure |
| act + ion | action | abrade + ion | abrasion |

Palatalization can, of course, happen across words as well as within words:

| | |
|---|---|
| dress your | 'dɹəʃɔ |
| what you | 'wɑʧə |
| ease your | 'iʒɔ |
| said your | 'sədʒə |

I call the name 'palatalization' infelicitous because (1) rarely does a sound resulting from this process become truly palatal (though you could argue that postalveolar is closer to palatal than alveolar is) and (2) [j] is already palatal and in fact can change to something less palatal. However, the term is well-established and will no doubt continue to be used.

| | |
|---|---|
| eʔkɑʃe̦ | Stkpt. 'it costs you' |
| ɹuuɪnʤə | ShB. 'ruined your' |
| kʊʤə | ShB. 'could you' |
| əʒ'jʊuʒʊ | Psmsh. 'as usual' |
| ɪtʃə'seɬf | Psmsh. '(mix) it yourself' |
| 'ənʤʊ | Psmsh. 'end, you (know)' |
| 'didn̩ʧə | Cov. 'didn't you' |
| wɔnʃjüud˺ | Nor. 'once you'd' |
| 'hɪʧ | Am. 'hit you' |
| 'æotʃə | Am. 'out you' |
| 'meɹiʤə | Am. 'married you' |
| 'juʒɚ | Am. 'use your' |
| 'faɪnʤɔ | SSB. 'find your' |
| wɒʧɔ | SSB. 'What you're' |
| 'ɬa:ʃɪə | Cov. 'last year' |
| 'dɨʤə | Nor. 'did you' |

## 2.6    Icons

At times, phrases which are used repeatedly reduce in ways which are extreme and not normally predicted by the forces suggested above. Examples are 'you know' and 'you know what I mean?' (approximately [jɔ̃] and [jɔ̃w̃ʌ̃mĩ], though these transcriptions are over-precise). As evidence of their lack of articulatory motivation, these highly-reduced forms are often locale-specific: the name of a town or an area will reduce dramatically simply because it is used so frequently. For example, at The Ohio State University, the icon for the institution is [hɐˈstɛɪʔ]. 'Cholmondeley' [ˈ ʧʌmlɪ] and 'Featherstonehaugh' [ˈfænʃɔ] are examples of this sort of idiosyncratic pronunciation, for which systematic explanations are difficult.

## 2.7    Weak Forms?

There is a small subset of English words which are short, frequent, and usually unstressed which behave much like unstressed syllables in longer words. What sets them apart is that they are entire words, albeit usually function words.

Most introductions to English phonology include a section on these 'weak' forms. These typically include what is abbreviated as 'll in 'I'll', 'you'll', as 'd in 'I'd', 'you'd', and as 've or 's in 'I've', 'you've', 'he's'.

While these forms admittedly have some idiosyncrasies, they are largely explainable using the principles set up above:

1    For the 've forms, you have loss of initial /h/, then the vowel, which is already reduced to schwa due to lack of stress, incorporates with the preceding vowel.
2    For the 'll forms, the situation is only slightly more complicated. Assuming that they are derived from an underlying 'will', we can again postulate vowel reduction, then an overlap of the resulting reduced vowel and approximate, as happens when the word 'were' is pronounced as a labialized schwa. The schwa

can then incorporate with the preceding vowel, as above. The apparent loss of labialization is not hard to understand, as the final velarized [l] induces similar lowering of higher formants and has itself a similar formant structure to a back rounded vowels. If we assume 'shall' as the underlying form which is said to weaken in the first person, the situation is not to be explained so simply. One could called upon regularization of the paradigm as an explanation, but this is always an unsatisfactory last resort, as it is impossible to explain why some irregular paradigms flourish while others don't.

3   For the 'd forms, another slight complication develops, as the weak form can stand for either 'had' or 'would'. Initial h-dropping and vowel incorporation can handle the former, but the loss of 'w' in 'would' remains unexplained by the processes above.

Some books on pronunciation include forms such as 'cn' (as in 'I cn do it') as weak forms. This has also been handled in the material above: the nasal consonant becomes syllabic as it overlaps with the schwa. Other words which often fall under the 'weak form' heading are pronouns starting with [h] and many other function words such as articles and frequent prepositions. All of these can be predicted using general principles, making it unnecessary to look at them case-by-case.

Cruttenden (2001: 254) points out that weak forms do not occur utterance-finally. This is probably the only case in which their status as full lexical items matters: presumably an utterance-final word will always receive enough stress to prevent reduction, though the same syllable will reduce finally if it is not a word in itself. ('A wonderful bird is the pelican; his bill can hold more than his belly can' (Merrit, 1910).)

Contractions of 'not' represent 'frozen' morphology, i.e. if the reductions associated with these forms were once active in English, they have now ceased to be productive. Nolan (1996: 19) makes a case for forms such as 'don't' being basic citation forms rather than being derived from their historical components (do + not in this case). As such it may qualify as a weak form or even an icon.

A pair of words which might be thought of as genuine weak forms in SSB. are 'Sir' and 'Saint', which are, unpredictably, [sə] and [sən] or [sn̩] (Cruttenden, 2001: 253). These words are markedly less stressed in SSB. than in some other varieties. They may also be thought of as iconic in the sense described above.

st. peter [sm̩pitə]
sir charles [səʧɑlz] or [ʂʧɑlz]

Hence, once stress placement and vowel centralization are understood, a large number of the other deviations from citation form which one finds in connected speech can be described using a small set of processes. It is often not necessary to consider weak forms as a separate case except in the sense that they are words rather than syllables within another word.

## 2.8   Combinations of these Processes

Each of the reductions discussed above seems trivial, and the application of any one of them to a phonological phrase is a very minor event. When several of them apply to the same citation form, the results can, however, be striking. Take, for example the citation form 'mountain' ['maʊntɨn] which can appear as [maʊʔn̩] after the application of schwa absorption, nasal incorporation and glottalling.

The sentence in the section on syllable shape above ('And the scientists . . .') is a good example of combined processes, as is Stampe's 'divinity fudge' in chapter 3: similar examples can be found in any unmonitored speech from the accents of English covered here.

# 3

# *Attempts at Phonological Explanation*

Since the beginning of the study of sound systems, phonologists have thought it their job to account for conditioned variation, i.e. variation in pronunciation brought about by some aspect of the linguistic environment which occurs whenever the relevant configuration arises. In casual speech, we encounter variation which is not entirely determined by linguistic features: we can find two or more variants in what appears to be exactly the same environment. Often this means that a potential conditioning factor is present but seems to exert no influence, so, for example, not all sequences of (unstressed vowel + nasal + voiceless stop) change to (nasalized vowel + stop). In this chapter, we examine attempts to deal with variation which is only partially predictable.

## 3.1   Past Work on Conversational Phonology

Quite a lot of previous work on unselfconscious speech has been done in a generative framework, as outlined below. Generative Phonology, and indeed any theory based on distinctive features, encounters an immediate problem with casual speech phonology: since the features involved are often not distinctive, writing rules is often not easy. Nasalization of vowels is relatively easy to characterize, since the feature [nasal] happens to also be distinctive. But rules involving glottal stops, taps, and many other sounds which play a part in casual speech but not in the system of oppositions bring in the use of invented features such as [ballistic] for tap. This tension between characterizing what is contrastive and expressing all regularities in the sound system cannot be resolved except by ad hoc means without a set of features designed to describe.systematic variants.

Units such as the syllable and especially the stressed syllable are not easily characterized in Generative Phonology. Stressed vowels can be identified, but consonants in stressed/unstressed syllables cannot (except as adjacent to a stressed/unstressed vowel). As stress affects consonants and vowels equally, theories which incorporate the notion of syllable (see Metrical Phonology, below) are more suitable for casual speech phonology.

With respect to variation, Generative Phonology held that pronunciation (or surface phonetic output) is derived from applying phonological rules to a set of basic underlying forms which are information-rich, i.e. they contain all the information needed to specify the contrasts in which a particular lexical item might be expected to participate. Phonological rules are thought of as reducing or permuting this basic information, causing neutralization, deletion, or insertion of information-free segments. A common view is expressed by Hooper (1976: 111):

> Any word or morpheme has a number of surface realisations predicted, not morphophonemically, but phonetically and by speech style or tempo. Furthermore, to the extent that the variation is predictable, it should be represented in the grammar . . . Variable representations of the same form are relatable to each other by general rules . . . The casual form may be derived from the careful form, but not vice-versa.

In this framework, each phonological rule, which can take an underlying form or the output of another rule as its input, has the potential to make a change in any form which meets its structural description. Variation is introduced through the optional rule: application is random or governed by extralinguistic or idiosyncratic factors and hence not predictable in a grammar.

Casual speech rules, then, were optional, though rules were thought to be triggered by increase in *rate*, and their outputs were thought to embody different *styles*. Harris (1969) recognizes four distinct varieties of educated Mexico City Spanish: Largo, Andante, Allegretto and Presto. They are defined as follows: Largo – very slow, deliberate, overprecise; Andante – moderately slow, careful, but natural; Allegretto – moderately fast, casual, colloquial; Presto – very fast, completely unguarded.

These strates (conflations of style and rate – my word, not from Harris) are distinguished by phonological criteria, e.g. with respect to nasals, 'In Largo, word-final -n does not assimilate to the initial consonant of the following word . . . Andante has partial assimilation across word boundaries . . . in Allegretto, distribution of nasals over word boundaries is precisely the same as that within words.' Clearly, not all rules will show distinct outputs at all four rates, but enough will do so to establish that four are necessary, hence strates are discrete and unambiguous. Presumably, a speech unit (phrase, sentence) will be uniform in its stratology and automatically assignable to one of his four categories.

Zwicky (1972a, b) appears to accept the notion 'fast = reduced' (though he points out that there are exceptions) and that there exist identifiable strates. Bolozky (1977) considers the question of whether recognizable strates are necessary in a theory of conversational phonology: they seem to be present in that people can identify speech as Lento or Allegro. Furthermore, he claims, some phonological rules apply only at more extreme rates, and this will have to be marked somewhere, so strates might be the answer. He tries to determine the number needed for English phonology. Dressler (1975) concludes that one might distinguish between a continuum of strates at the phonetic level and a discrete number at a phonological level, though the rules for doing so are not divulged.

Shockey (1974) suggests that, though impressionistic judgments about style and rate may be consistent, it is very unlikely that uniform strates can be identified on the basis of application of phonological rules. There is some correlation between increased rate and degree of reduction, but the relationship is far from straightforward. Given two productions of the same sequence of words, one fast, one slow, the faster one will probably show more reduction, but not always in such a way that you could regard the slower version as an input to some rules which will produce the faster version. (I.e. conversion rules could be written, but would have no generality.)

Two examples:

'and it's non-repayable'    slower [ɛ̃ɪsnən,ɪpɛɪʰbl̩]
                            faster [ɛ̃nɪsnəɹɪpʰɛɪbl̩]

'you couldn't relax'        slower [jʉkʰʊdn̩ɹɪ'læks]
                            faster [jʉkʰʊntɹɪ'læks]

In the first, we see only a nasalized vowel for 'and' in the slower version, but a fully realized nasal in the faster. In the second, we see different treatment of the underlying [kʊdn̩t].

## 3.2    Natural Phonology

Stampe, a phonologist who has been concerned with casual speech since the 1960s, has a sort of reversal of perspective on the problem: he thinks that acquisition of language, like acquisition of other skills, is a process of *suppressing* some of the behaviour which is present in all normal humans. For example, young babies can and do make every vowel sound possible for their vocal tracts. As they acquire their environmental language(s), they suppress some vowels in favour of others and eventually develop a system /systems equivalent to their model(s).

The suppression of natural processes can also be called upon to explain variation in adult phonology. If we assume that higher degrees of repression facilitate greater degrees of precision (and hence enlarge our ability to produce statistically uncommon forms), we must conclude that slow, formal, maximally-differentiated speech is the peak of repression. Other speech strates would then involve relaxation of suppression, or movement towards a more natural situation. This theory provides a principled explanation of why reductions seem to be more generalized in casual speech than in formal speech: they would always apply unless restricted from doing so.

This means that instead of having new rules of casual speech, you can view its production as switching off some of the rules used in formal speech. Dressler (1975) and Bailey support this view to various degrees, but Hooper (1976: 114) criticizes it on the grounds that there is no principled way to discover which forms are more natural and which more repressed. For example, with a target /ti/, which output is more natural, [ti] or [ʧi]?

Stampe's theory supports the intuition that one is doing less work in casual speech rather than more, though the mapping between physical relaxation and phonological relaxation is not always obvious.

## 3.3 Variable Rules

The question of strates is very wisely avoided by the Variationists, whose work is based on that of William Labov, the father of the variable rule (1969). In this framework, the application (or non-application) of a rule is governed by the linguistic, sociological, and psychological environment in which an utterance is produced. E.g., optional rules are not really optional, but are almost completely deterministic (leaving some room for idiosycracies). Cedargren and Sankoff (1974) extended the theory to include probabilities: the presence or absence of a particular factor or configuration of factors affects the probability that a rule will apply. As might be imagined, the resulting calculation can be very complex. (See Fasold, 1990: 244ff for an illustration of this approach.)

Bailey (1973) attempted to account for variation within the speech strates of one speaker as well as variation over time and across accents by (1) changes in marking of distinctive features (from, say, marked to unmarked or from heavily weighted to less heavily weighted) and (2) reordering of phonological rules to more natural or unmarked orders. Bailey, like Stampe and Hooper, sees phonological rules as operating in a natural fashion, i.e. not random, but moving in a direction which allows humans to use their production and perception abilities maximally. He says (p. 41), 'Linguistic analyses marking feature coefficients instead of static pluses and minuses have directional change built into them.' He compares his work to that of Cedargren and Sankoff on the grounds that his feature weightings can be associated with the probabilistic linguistic functions which these authors see as governing variability.

The variable rule has been criticized and, in fact, has been virtually discarded by mainstream phonologists, on two grounds: (1) probabilities of application of a particular rule are a feature of an accent group rather than an individual. The relationship between the language behaviour of a community and the mental grammar of an individual is unknown and probably unknowable. How could an individual keep track of the percentages of rule application in their own production so as to be sure to match the group? If, indeed, this is possible, is it part of the grammar? (2) Linguistic theories are by nature abstract and are about how constrast is achieved (hence meaning conveyed) in particular circumstances. Number of outputs of any particular type is of no interest whatsoever. Pierrehumbert (1994) counterargues, however, that variation is intrinsic to the nature of language and therefore should be intrinsic to our scientific study of language. The options offered by Trace or Event Theory, outlined below, may satisfy her argument without too much computational apparatus.

## 3.4   More on Rule Order

It has been noted that there is a negative implicational relationship among the phonological rules concerned in conversational speech: rule X may not apply unless rule W has already applied. Hooper comments, (p. 112) '. . . in the word **security**, it is possible to have an output to which flapping has been applied, but not schwa deletion: [sˈkjɚɨɾi]; but an unacceptable output results from applying schwa deletion without applying flapping, *[sˈkjɚɨti].' She later continues (p. 113), 'If we think of the styles in a hierarchy, the most explicit style being the highest and the most casual style being the lowest, we find that the reflexes of rules that apply in a higher style are never undone in a lower style.' Hence, though Hooper is not an advocate of the explicit ordering of phonological rules, she suggests that there is some directionality in their application.

While an advocate of ordered processes in the phonology of individuals (1979: 16), Stampe says that processes apply in a 'random, nonlinear, sequential way' (p. 60) with the derivation of the words 'divinity fudge' (nougat) put forth as evidence:

| | |
|---|---|
| other processes | *dəˈvɪnəti ˈfʌdʒ |
| syllabification | *də.ˈvɪn.ə.ti ˈfʌdʒ |
| flapping | *də.ˈvɪɾ̃.ə.ti ˈfʌdʒ |
| vowel nasalization | də.ˈvĩɾ̃.ə.ti ˈfʌdʒ |
| flap deletion | də.ˈvĩə̃.ti ˈfʌdʒ |
| syllabification | *də.ˈvĩ.ə.ti ˈfʌdʒ |
| vowel nasalization | də.ˈvĩĩ.ti ˈfʌdʒ |
| schwa-harmony | də.ˈvĩə̃.ti ˈfʌdʒ |
| shortening | də.ˈvĩ.ti ˈfʌdʒ |
| syllabification | ˇdə.ˈvɪt.i ˈfʌdʒ |
| flapping | də.ˈvɪɾ.i ˈfʌdʒ |
| flap-nasalization | də.ˈvɪɾ̃.i ˈfʌdʒ |
| flap-deletion | də.ˈvĩ.i ˈfʌdʒ |
| syllabification | *də.ˈvĩi ˈfʌdʒ |
| vowel nasalization | də.ˈvĩĩ ˈfʌdʒ |

(*Marks 'unpronounceable items'. I interpret 'unpronounceable' to mean 'not accepted American vernacular' here, as the starred sequences are clearly pronounceable in the strictest sense.)

He comments (p. 59) that this derivation does not exhaust the possible pronunciations of the phrase, nor is it the most extreme reduction possible. He adds, 'The asterisks mark forms which are not pronounceable because there are obligatory substitutions which have not applied', which also implies directionality – an interlinking of sets of phonological rules (or processes). We cannot review the complex arguments over whether rules should be ordered here, but it is interesting to note the idea that often several casual speech rules or processes are thought to work together in well-defined combinations in order to generate only those pronunciations which are current in the relaxed speech of a particular community, though others might be permitted by the rules themselves. This interlinking would, in Hooper's view, prevent forms such as [ʂˈkjɚti] from being generated or, in Stampe's view, guarantee that other rules applied to this form obligatorily to prevent unconventional pronunciations. (Clearly, these links are accent-specific, since [sˈkjʌɹti] is perfectly acceptable in British English.).

Stampe rejects the notion that casual speech processes can be attributed to inertial properties of the vocal tract: for him, phonological processes are purely mental. Hooper's example supports this notion, for if the sole purpose of casual phonology is to increase ease of articulation, why should some forms be prevented from occurring? Presumably, [ʂˈkjʌɹɨɾi] is easier to say than [sɨkjʌɹɨɾi] because the former has no voicing in the first syllable: the extra vocal cord adjustments are not necessary. The form does not occur because of the linguistic habits of speakers of American English, which are governed by mental processes. Stampe argues that processes are mental in origin, physical in teleology: their purpose is to maximize the perceptual characteristics of speech and to minimize its articulatory difficulties (1979: 9).

For more explanation of Natural Phonology see Donegan and Stampe (1979) and Dressler (1984).

## 3.5   Attempts in the 1990s

### 3.5.1   *Autosegmental*

Autosegmental Phonology (Goldsmith, 1990) has its roots in the study of tone languages, where tone can be said to be a property of syllables (or even sequences of syllables) rather than segments.

The autosegmental approach makes describing quite a few conversational processes much easier than the classical generative approach. It assumes that there is a basic representation of a phonological string which consists of either consonant (C) or vowel (V) slots. Each of these slots is linked to the features which describe its articulation by a set of association lines. There is an association line to each relevant feature. In order to describe changes from the base form, you can make associations to new features (adding association lines) or cut association lines which are already there. If you cut all associations to a slot in the CV string, it is simply not pronounced. Association lines must not cross.

Let's take, for example, the process whereby a VN sequence becomes a nasalized vowel in words like [kɑ̃t] 'can't' as mentioned above. We start with the CV structure:

where there is an association line between the segment marked 'n' and the feature *nasal*. At the beginning, the vowel is not linked to the nasal feature, but it is possible to draw an association line which links the vowel to *nasal* as well, and thus the spread of nasality can be shown. If the nasal consonant does not show closure, the association lines to the consonantal features of the segment can be cut.

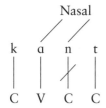

If the nasalized vowel takes up the duration of the original VN sequence, association lines between the C slot and the features of the previous vowel can be drawn. An apparent anomaly can thus be created in that a consonantal slot is not linked to any consonantal features, but presumably this is the mechanism by which compensatory lengthening must be explained. (Some versions of the mechanism simply use 'X' to mark the slot, so no commitment to V or C is suggested.)

In common with the generative approach, this does not handle situations where a segment is only *partially* nasalized, voiced, devoiced, etc.

This approach allows for assimilation, deletion and overlap of the type seen above. The addition of new segments such as those which appear between nasals and homorganic stops in words like 'prince' and 'hamster' is be harder to deal with, but these are not, in fact, phonological segments and it would probably be a mistake to explain them phonologically.

For further information on this theory, see Goldsmith (1990).

### 3.5.2   Metrical

Standard generative phonology did not deal in syllables or other potentially submorphemic units, so had problems accommodating stress and rhythm. The metrical approach (Liberman, 1975; Nespor and Vogel, 1986) is oriented towards describing/explaining just these aspects of language. Conversational speech processes, as we have seen, are strongly influenced by degree of stress in a phrase, so a theory which allows us to predict this will allow us to predict degree of reduction, not only of vowels, but of consonant force. Metrical phonology provides a way of indicating both syllable boundaries and syllable structures, and this is very important for conversational phonology: syllable-initial segments (onset) and syllable final (especially word-final) (coda) segments differ very significantly in their behaviour in conversational speech, as we have observed in chapter 2. A version of metrical phonology is fully integrated into Optimality Theory (section 3.5.6).

### 3.5.3   Articulatory

Articulatory phonology (Browman and Goldstein 1986, 1990, 1992) assumes that lexical items are represented in the brain as sets of instructions to the articulators (hence, it would appear, uniting phonetics and phonology completely). The question of whether the traditional phonological system exists and if so where and how is not addressed.

Each utterance consists of a series of gestures. When speech is articulated, the gestures overlap, and this accounts for effects such as vowels nasalizing before nasals and other simple assimilatory processes. A gesture always takes the same amount of time, so gestures can vary only in amplitude and degree of overlap. If one speaks faster, the gestures overlap more, hence we expect more coarticulation. If gestures overlap completely (and especially if one gesture is attenuated), it can appear that a segment has been deleted, but Browman and Goldstein argue that no such deletion is possible – the gestures are simply indistinguishable from each other because they begin and end at the same time. Gestural phonology is better than most others at explaining timing. Most phonological theories operate in a time-free zone: this one does not because it explicitly relates abstract segments to their manner of production (i.e. the conflation of phonetics and phonology requires the introduction of timing into phonology). It is not tied to segment boundaries, so can explain partial nasalization or partial devoicing of, for example, a vowel. Autosegmental phonology can re-link association lines to provide a totally new pronunciation of any particular segment, but gestural phonology has difficulty in accommodating articulatory substitutions which introduce elements not normally considered to belong to the original target. (An example might be Birmingham [gɛɹʊp] for 'get up', where [t] and [ɹ] are not simply a stop/approximant version of the same gesture. According to Pierrehumbert (1994), 'The low third formant characteristic of /r/ is achievable by lip rounding, raising the tongue blade, or a constriction in the pharyngeal region; different speakers do, in fact, use different methods of producing /r/.') Kohler (1992) argues that gestural overlap cannot account for all phonological changes in German. He suggests that gestural reorganization is necessary in some cases.

For further exposition on the gestural approach, see Browman and Goldstein (1986, 1992).

### 3.5.4   *Underspecification*

We have observed that (1) syllable-final alveolar sounds are especially volatile, but that (2) syllable-initially they are stable. It has been suggested (Paradis and Prunet, 1989, 1991; Lodge, 1992) that (1) can be traced to the fact that syllable-final coronals are not fully specified for place of articulation in the underlying representation. Place features are consequently assigned by linguistic attributes of their environment with dental/alveolar as a default value, i.e. the one which is assumed if no other feature takes over. 'Spreading' occurs when a feature fills an underspecified slot in an adjacent unit. Lodge (p. 25) suggests that (2) is true because subsystems within a language can undergo different processes: onset position conditions the early specification of place for coronals, whereas coda position does not.

In addition Lodge also assumes (p. 28) that /ð/ is underspecified for manner, since it retains its place but can assimilate in manner to preceding consonants.

### 3.5.5   Firthian prosodics

Several linguists (Kelly and Local, 1989; Simpson, 1992; Ogden, 1999) advocate an approach which they describe as a development from the theories of J. R. Firth (1957). According to these researchers, phonology is done at an abstract ('algebraic') level, and everything else is phonetics. This technique maps directly from citation form to surface form without attributing any special significance to the phoneme or any other abstractly-defined unit. Given a string of lexical items in citation form, it assigns features to portions of an utterance, resulting in a nasalized, labialized, or otherwise phonetically realized section which does not necessarily correspond to an even number of underlying phonological units. An important assumption here is that there is no significant structural change in the spoken form: the citation form is produced or performed using components which decide its phonetic identity. Some performances may have little or no acoustic reflex of particular phonological units as a result of the way the prosodies interact. A useful analogy might be with stops on an organ which allow the input musical patterns to be realized in different ways and which can be switched in and out at independent intervals, even in the middle of a note. (If these prosodies are thought of as gestures, there is considerable superficial similarity to the articulatory approach, outlined above.) The analogy with music fails when it comes to timing: the abstract, algebraic form is timeless, and duration can be assigned like any other prosody, so phonology is time-free but phonetics is not. This means that the timing of phonetic effects can overlap in different ways, and this can lead to perceptual impressions such as tapping of alveolar obstruents or epenthetic stops in words such as 'ham(p)ster'. This approach has been used effectively in speech synthesis (Coleman, 1994; Dirksen and Coleman, 1994; Local and Ogden, 1997).

Another major tenet of this theory is that different phonological systems can exist in different environments/linguistic domains, so that, e.g. syllable-initial and syllable-final consonants would not necessarily be expected to show similar phonological behaviour (as, indeed, they do not), nor would content and function words.

While most processes discussed in this book (for example devoicing, schwa incorporation, nasal displacement and tapping) can be accounted for using the Firthian approach, sounds which appear to be deleted entirely create a problem, as mentioned for Gestural Phonology, above: if they were really deleted, it would involve restructuring the input forms, which is not permitted. I say 'appear to be deleted' because it would be possible to argue that the units/gestures are not deleted but simply performed in such a way that one or more of them has/have no acoustic consequences. The difference between being deleted and being fully attenuated must then be made clear.

For more on the Firthian approach, see Langendoen (1968), Lass (1984, ch. 10), Ogden (1999).

### 3.5.6   Optimality Theory

Optimality theory (OT) claims that there are certain universal constraints which are the raw material for phonologies of all languages. Like Stampe's natural processes, they include notions of statistical frequency: in general, the more common a phonological process is, the more powerful. Power is expressed in terms of ranking – while all constraints are violable, higher-ranked constraints are less violable than lower-ranked ones. 'No Voicing in Final Obstruents', for example, is ranked highly in most languages. Languages (or accents) have different phonologies because rankings are different from language to language.

OT suggests that there is a language-independent device which generates all possible pronunciation candidates for a lexical item.

The language-specific phonological grid (in which the ranking of the constraints is listed) filters out all candidates but one, the output.

For a more detailed introduction, see Roca and Johnson, (1999, ch. 19).

## Variation

The major problem in using OT for casual speech phonology is that while variation *across* accents can be described, variation *within* an accent is (at first glance) impossible to describe because there is a single mapping between the lexical input and the phonetic output. The ranked constraints determine which of the input forms is the winner, and there is only one winner.

Kager (1999) suggests two possible solutions: (1) variants are the result of different phonologies, such that Variant A is generated by Grid A while Variant B is generated by Grid B. In his words, 'an input can be fed into two parallel co-phonologies, giving two outputs' (p. 405). This, he admits, is a ponderous solution to a simple problem. (Nathan (1988) suggests that these co-phonologies may be styles, such that different speech styles have different phonologies.) (2) Variants are caused by variable ranking of constraints, such that two constraints can be ranked AB on one occasion and BA on another. In his words, 'Evaluation of the candidate set is split into two subhierarchies, each of which selects an optimal candidate.' This is known as *free ranking* (Prince and Smolensky, 1993).

Kager joins Guy (1997) in preferring the second option; Guy because Occams Razor argues against such a general duplication of constructs, Kager because it links the amount of 'free variation' in the (single) grammar with the number of free-ranked constraints. In the multiphonology option, there is no necessary connection between the two (or more) grammars needed to generate two or more outputs from the same input.

In agreement with Anttila (1997), Kager also points out that the notion of *preferred* versus *unpreferred ranking* allows us the possibility of predicting which of the two outputs will be more frequent. This is a major improvement over the optional rule of generative phonology, which we have assumed applied randomly. However, it is otherwise identical to the optional rule, and the notion of preferred versus unpreferred application would have made the same improvement to the older theory. Nathan (1988) points out yet another problem: there may be three, four, or even more casual speech outputs from the same input (as demonstrated in Natural Phonology, above), which makes adequate constraint ranking a very complex business.

Boersma (1998, ch. 15) carries constraint ranking further in proposing an OT grammar in which constraints are ranked probabilistically rather than absolutely. Kager (1999: 407) sums up this approach: 'Fine-tuning of free variation may be achieved by associating a freely-ranked constraint with a numerical index indicating its relative strength with respect to all other constraints. This may pave the way to a probabilistic view of constraint inter-action.' Boersma claims (p. 330) that the flexibility offered by such a grammar can shed light on the acquisition of phonology by children and the ability to understand unfamiliar accents in adults: listeners learn to match the degree of optionality of their language environment. This approach is, of course, subject to the same criti-cisms made of Labov and the Variationists with respect to whether probabilities are a valid part of grammar.

### Glottal stopping in a modified OT framework

In an OT framework, we have a principled way to represent the fact that different accents of English share casual speech features but differ in the extent to which these features appear on the surface. SSB., for example, normally allows glottal stopping of /t/ only in syllable-final position when followed by a consonant or silence. Some accents allow it intervocalically. Surface forms (such as ['bʌʔə] for 'butter') are thus included in Cockney and some English Midland accents. We could say this is because they rank Glottal Stopping before Unstressed Onset Faithfulness (adherence to the lexical form at the beginning of unstressed syllables).

Kerswill (personal communication, 2001) reports that there is an accent in Durham (northern England) in which sequences such as [sɛvn̩'ʔaɪmz] 'seven times' are legal. Glottal Stopping could thus be said to outrank both Stressed and Unstressed Onset Faithfulness in this accent. There are undoubtedly other accents which constrain the process in yet other ways.

Following is a proposed phonological grid in the style of OT. (There is no information here about environments in which the output can be found or frequency of occurrence of each variant, as would be called for in an adequate phonological account of the accents.)

I say 'in the style of OT' because the grid has been modified to allow for variation (indicated by ☉). A frown (☹) indicates that a form is possible but not preferred, and an exclamation mark (!) shows that a form is impossible in this accent. Otherwise, the forms listed are acceptable.

'Faithfulness' means that the output matches the input. I assume here that the constraint which preserves the citation form at the beginning of stressed syllables is different from the one which performs a similar function for unstressed syllables: we have observed elsewhere that stressed onsets have a special status.

Moving down from the top of figure 3.1 (SSB.) to the bottom (Durham), we see that as faithfulness to the lexical form becomes less constraining, glottal-stopping occurs in more environments, and variability becomes greater because the 'faithful' pronunciation remains a possibility.

Other casual speech processes such as tapping also lend themselves nicely to description in an OT framework. Hammond (Archangeli et al., 1998: 46) describes some aspects of schwa absorption using OT, but is limited by notions of 'fast speech' and by a very small data set.

### 3.5.7    A synthesist

One phonetician/phonologist collects, transcribes, and attempts to provide phonological explanations for casual speech in several different accents of British English and is in the process of developing a composite phonological theory. Lodge (1984) assumes 'that English is subject to a number of widespread phonological processes. Many of these have been recurrent throughout its history and some have been continuing for a century or more . . . However, these

**SSB.**

| Stressed onset faithfulness | Unstressed onset faithfulness | Lose oral closure /t/ | Other |
|---|---|---|---|
| 'seven times' | | | |
| sɛvən taɪmz | | !sɛvən ʔaɪmz | |
| 'butter' | | | |
| | bʌtə | ⊗bʌʔə | |
| 'cat' | | | |
| ⊙ | | kæʔ | kæt |

**Cockney, Midlands**

| Stressed onset faithfulness | Lose oral closure /t/ | Unstressed onset faithfulness | Other |
|---|---|---|---|
| 'seven times' | | | |
| sɛvən taɪmz | !sɛvən ʔaɪmz | | |
| 'butter' | | | |
| ⊙ | bʌʔə | bʌtə | |
| 'cat' | | | |
| ⊙ | kæʔ | | kæt |

**Durham**

| Lose oral closure /t/ | Stressed onset faithfulness | Unstressed onset faithfulness | Other |
|---|---|---|---|
| 'seven times' | | | |
| ⊙ sɛvən ʔaɪmz | sɛvən taɪmz | | |
| 'butter' | | | |
| ⊙ bʌʔə | | bʌtə | |
| 'cat' | | | |
| ⊙ kæʔ | | | kæt |

*Figure 3.1* t-glottalling in several accents

processes are not distributed uniformly . . . and I hope to show how the different distribution of the processes helps to distinguish between the different accents' (p. 5). He adds, 'The present book is intended as a contribution to determine what all English accents do have in common and what distinguishes them from one another' (p. 18).

He attributes such processes as lenition, harmony (a wider term than 'assimilation' which incorporates assimilation (including [ə]-assimilation) vowel harmony and palatalization), cluster simplification, nasal incorporation, glottalling, and glottal reinforcement to his six accents of British English.

Lodge's book is couched largely in terms of Dependency Phonology (Anderson and Jones, 1977; Anderson and Ewen, 1980), as is an earlier paper (1981) in which he makes several provocative suggestions such as (1) that preconsonantal and prepausal /t/ is underlyingly a glottal gesture (or phonation type) which receives its surface form from its phonetic environment or, if there is none, appears on the surface as a glottal stop; and (2) the second element in some final consonant clusters is more likely than the first to drop out because the second consonant is dependent on the first but not vice versa.

Point (1) above is taken up again (1992, 1995) in a discussion of underspecification. The notion here is that features which are contextually determined do not have to be specified in deep structure: features can be copied from surrounding elements, making it unnecessary to create rules or processes to change fully specified underlying features. Properties can spread through 'transparent' segments without changing them and to underspecified segments. [ð], for example, has no underlying 'place' specification in this framework because its place varies depending on the previous consonant.

Lodge uses elements of autosegmental phonology in that tiers are necessary to relate phonological representations to phonetic forms, but in later work (1993, 1997) he decides against segment-level phonology while retaining the tiers. His later work is done in a declarative framework, using two aspects of the Firthian approach: polysystematicity (which means that different phonological systems can be in operation in different parts of a linguistic unit – for example, syllable-initially and syllable finally) and the prosody, i.e. linguistically-significant effects which can be present for a syllable or more. He gives the example of German 'bat' versus 'Bart': in the latter, there is no measurable separate 'r' segment – rather, the whole word is more velarized than the former. (Presumably, General American 'hot' and 'heart' would differ in an analogous way, though the prosody is different.) In this respect, he follows the Firthian school mentioned above and in fact has written jointly with this group (Local and Lodge, 1996).

## 3.6   And into the New Millennium

### 3.6.1   Trace/Event theory

Until recently, many theories of speech perception assumed that acoustic input was matched to an invariant lexical representation through normalization. Variation in the speech signal brought about by head size, voice type, rate, style, or accent have been thought to be filtered out or eliminated, allowing the perceiver to arrive at the more abstract phonological values of the linguistic units.

Researchers have challenged this theory both historically (Semon, quoted in Goldringer, 1997) and recently (other authors in Johnson and Mullinix, 1997; Jusczyk, 1997). Their experiments demonstrate that perceptual tokens which have been heard/seen previously are easier to perceive than unfamiliar ones. This suggests that information such as voice type and other features mentioned above (sometimes called 'indexical' information) is stored along with the linguistic bare bones in the recognition lexicon.

Jusczyk (1997: 206ff) hypothesizes that when a human child first hears a word, it creates a new entry in its lexicon which is, limitations of the hearing mechanism aside, acoustic. There are no linguistic subdivisions or attempts to assign internal structure to the word, there is no processing which filters out indexical information, it is simply stored as a piece of sound with whatever meaning the child is able to assign to it. This acoustic unit is a 'trace'. Subsequent hearings of a word recognized as the same are stored in the same location, so that after some experience with the language, each lexical entry consists of a number of traces. Portions of the lexical item which are consistently present are more highly reinforced than portions which are not, so presumably some portions come to be seen as more essential than others.

This means that variants which we have thought of above as being linked through some phononological process such as tapping or vowel devoicing are actually present simultaneously as traces in the lexical entry and are recognized as the same through having the same meaning.

Docherty and Foulkes (2000), remark that it would seem highly uneconomic to assume that the recognition lexicon and the phonological lexicon are different. If traces rather than phonemic-sized units are the basis of phonological representation, how do phonological constructs such as the phoneme and the syllable and its subparts emerge in the individual lexicon, if at all? As Shankweiler and Crain (1986: 42) point out, 'explicit conscious awareness of phonemic structures depends on metalinguistic abilities that do not come free with the acquisition of language.' Many four- and five-year-old children with otherwise normal language skills are unable to count the number of phonemes in a spoken word and cannot identify words which do not rhyme with other words (Tunmer and Rohl, 1991: 2). Fowler (1991) suggests, however, that phoneme awareness grows gradually between the ages of 3 and 7, and, Mann (1991: 202–4) agrees that a certain amount of phoneme awareness develops naturally with age and is found in Japanese nine-year-olds who have not had experience with an alphabetic writing system. She adds (p. 210) that, counter to Tunmer and Rohl's findings, some kindergarten children who cannot read perform well on tasks that require the manipulation of phonemes and can invent spellings that capture the phonetic structure of spoken words. Earlier work by Lundberg, Olofsson, and Wall (1980) presages these results.

Presumably, familiar lexical entries are based primarily on acoustic information in a very young language user, but are joined by traces of their written form when the user becomes literate, so traces can be orthographic as well as auditory. Tunmer and Rohl also observe (1991: 17) that though some metalinguistic skills in segmenting words into phonemes is necessary in learning to read, the acquisition of reading skills can in turn improve performance on phonological awareness tasks. So we can assume that traces from different senses can reinforce each other: evidence for the opposite certainly exists – 'what distinguishes . . . the nonreader from the successful reader is the specific failure to access the phoneme' (Fowler, 1991: 100). Furthermore, poor readers of all ages show deficits in naming pictures of familiar objects, suggesting that their lexical representations are less precisely specified than those of good readers (p. 101).

The acquisition of letter-to-sound rules can then further allow new entries to be created by the reader (sometimes in error, leading to spelling pronunciations such as ['vɪk tʃuəlz] for ['vɪtlz]). These rules also allow the reading of nonce words and non-words which presumably do not flourish in the lexicon as a result of lack of stimulation.

In agreement (however accidental) with Stampe (1979, 1987), Mann (1991: 207) notes that knowledge of the alphabet is not the only factor that determines phoneme awareness. Language games along the lines of 'pig Latin' (where a word like 'bee' becomes 'eebay' with the exchange of the onset and coda and the insertion of [ei]) are played in a wide range of languages, many of which do not have alphabetic writing systems. Players include young children and illiterates, who could not participate without implicit knowlege of the phonemic principle in many of her examples. She adds (p. 209), however, that these games are easier for people who have acquired an alphabetic system.

One might further propose that phonemic consciousness is a byproduct of comparing different traces within a location as well as across locations. If, for example, [bænd] and [bæn] are alternative pronunciations of the same word, the [d] must be a separable unit. And if [bænd] and [sænd] are different words, the [b] and the [s] must be separable items. If so, the phonemic system is a product of the lexicon rather than the converse.

The fact that traces retain their indexical information and are not essentially segmental suggests a route for learning to recognize and produce different speech styles and/or for learning to understand and imitate accents not one's own: long-term vocal tract settings could, for example, be represented as traces. (Work by

Weil (2001) suggests, however, that these long-term settings are recognizable only in utterances longer than a single word.)

To what degree these powers of abstraction can be attributed to language users is under debate, but we could easily imagine a complete restructuring of an individual's mental lexicon upon their discovering that, say, there is a systematic distinction between 'p' and 'b' or that 'ment' is a suffix. If this were to happen in stages during the mastery of one's native language, the lexicon of an observant and experienced language user could have a form similar to that of a dictionary, with phonemes, stems, and affixes represented. Bybee states firmly (2000a: 82) ' "Phonemes" do not exist as units [in the lexicon]; the phenomena that phonemes are intended to describe are relations of similarity among parts of the phonetic string.' She also notes (2000b: 253) that traces do not distinguish between phonetic and phonological forms. It seems necessary, however, to have an internal representation consisting of traces *and* whatever linguistic constructs have been abstracted in order to account for the phonemic awareness in children and illiterates discussed above. People will differ in their ability to make abstractions from lexical entries, which is likely to be correlated with differences in reading and spelling ability.

In this approach to describing phonological behaviour the phonemic inventory and the morphology are derived from the lexicon: small units are products of big units rather than the converse. This makes any linkage with traditional phonological approaches difficult, though presumably not impossible.

The trace model is attractive in that it attempts to unite what we know about human language behaviour with cognitive representation and in that it can allow for unconditioned variation in a straightforward manner (cf. Al-Tamimi, 2002). In common with Gestural and Prosodic Phonology, it also provides a rationale for the otherwise mysterious fact that native perceivers of a language recognize reduced sequences as if they were not reduced at all. We recognize a three-legged dog as still a dog, but with something missing. One might expect us to have a similar percept of a word with missing bits, but we recognize the 'ham' in 'hambag' as a realization of the word 'hand' as if it were fully articulated. In some sense, the citation form is firmly in the message: the spoken version is transparent. Perhaps this is because, as these theories suggest, full and reduced forms are always simultaneously present in the minds of the users.

## 3.7   Summary

Early attempts at describing casual speech used optional rules, which seem to apply randomly, and variable rules the application of which is based on sociological variables to account for unconditioned variation. Some regarded rate and style as the main factor governing their application. Later work attributes them to vocal tract inertia, gestural overlap, and/or the non-suppression of natural processes.

Gestural and Prosodic Phonology share the notion that the underlying representation is not radically restructured by the articulation process. They are sceptical whether underlying elements which appear to have no phonetic manifestation actually undergo a process of deletion or simply cannot be heard, though it is not clear whether these actually amount to entirely different things.

'Trace' or 'Event' Theory assumes that our lexical representations are an accretion of tokens of lexical items which have been perceived by an individual (presumably in any perceptual mode). Since this accretion includes all pronunciations, variation of all sorts is built into the model. More abstract aspects of phonology such as knowledge of the phonemic system are, however, not explained. In general, theories which are good at characterizing abstract phonological systems are not good at characterizing casual speech processes and vice versa.

Looking back at chapter 2, we must not forget that many of the conditioning factors for phonological reduction lie in factors outside phonology, and the interaction of these factors (morphology, syntax, semantics, pragmatics, discourse structure) with phonology must be a concern of anyone interested in explanatory adequacy. While these interactions (especially that with morphology) have not been ignored, neither have they been fully explored.

# 4

# Experimental Studies in Casual Speech

Deciding which research can be said to contribute to an understanding of casual speech is not easy: much of what has been done on speech anatomy and physiology has contributed to our understanding of the physical and neurological constraints on the vocal tract which are, in turn, reflected in casual speech processes. Studies on coarticulation, stress, syllable production, timing, and rate as well as on general phonetic and phonological theory have all provided insights. Much of the research in speech perception is just as applicable to casual speech as to other kinds. As we cannot attempt an overview of experimental phonetics/phonology, this chapter will review research on both speech production and speech perception by those who have intentionally investigated casual, unselfconscious speech, with the goal of looking at what is known about the processes discussed in chapter 2.

## 4.1 Production of Casual Speech

### 4.1.1 General production studies

#### Impressionistic

Some studies of the production of unmonitored speech are based on impressionistic observation and/or intuition. These generally consist of phonetic transcription of live or recorded data.

Just as it is impossible to list all forebears in experimental linguistics, it would be impossible to list all of the work done on varieties of spoken English in the sociolinguistic literature, most of which is impressionistic. Too many descriptions of English accents to mention here contain information about casual speech reductions, but combined with more general information on monitored or citation-form pronunciation. In this work, we take it for granted that all spoken language is produced under sociolinguistic influences but do not attempt to quantify these influences, nor can we hope to survey the massive body of writing on the sociolinguistics of the many varieties of English.

Brown (1977, 1996) reports having heard a large number of the processes discussed in chapter 2 in the speech of newscasters. Among these are schwa absorption, intervocalic weakening of obstruents, and final t/d deletion. Her book is aimed at teachers of English as a foreign language, and her message is that students will never understand English if they are taught only citation forms. (See chapter 5 for more about her work.)

Lodge's (1984) summary of processes present in several accents of British English focuses on informal speech. His conclusions agree in general with what is said in chapter 2 about [ð]-assimilation, glottalling, nasal replacement, and palatalization. He attempts to formulate a phonological framework which can accommodate English casual speech which is discussed briefly in chapter 3 of this book.

### Augmented transcription

Another body of research has supplemented phonetic transcription with acoustic displays, usually spectrograms. Dalby's (1984) study of Am. fast speech was aimed at discovering whether unstressed vowel reduction occurs more frequently as speech rate increases. He concluded that rate interacts with other factors such as position in word and number and type of segments adjacent to the unstressed vowel and proposed a model in which the syllable structure of the citation form played a large role to account for these complex interactions.

Shockey's (1974) dissertation attempts to come to grips with whether more phonological reduction occurs in unselfconscious casual speech than in speech read from a script. I found that in Am., while there was some evidence for the notion that read speech was less reduced, unscripted and scripted speech show very great phonological similarity: the same processes apply and very nearly to the same degree. I concluded that the majority of phonological processes cannot be used as style markers since they are not under conscious control. Speakers do not know that they are producing speech which differs from citation form, and, in fact, deny it when asked. (cf. Brown, 1977: 55). Nolan and Cobb (1994) discovered, however, that while subjects may not be aware of their own or others' casual speech reductions *per se*, they can make consistent judgements about the level of casualness in language spoken by others, suggesting that there are different levels of awareness of these processes.

I found that using spectrograms as corroboration of one's pho-netic transcription is a sobering and enlightening experience, es-pecially when working with one's own native language: the phonemic interpretation of the spoken material emerges as the default percept if the transcriber's attention wanders even for a moment. This is the case even for very experienced phoneticians. Needless to say, the phonemic interpretation can be unhelpful and even completely wrong phonetically, and the acoustic displays force the transcriber to justify each symbol used. The results of my study are reflected in chapter 2.

## Spectrography

Lindblom's (1990) H&H Theory holds that as speech becomes hypo- (under) articulated, targets are not realized as fully as in a more monitored hyper- (over) articulated style, hence there is more coarticulation between and among segments. A method of testing this hypothesis was used by Krull. Based on work by Lindblom (1963) and Sussman (1991), she assumes that formant frequencies at the CV boundary are affected by the articulation of the con-sonant, as are F2 (second formant) maxima or minima in the vowel. She calls the F2 value at the C-V boundary the 'locus' and plots the difference between the locus and the maximal or minimal F2 value of the following vowel (the turning point). If the locus and the turning point are the same, there is said to be maximal coarticulation. As the difference becomes greater, the coarticulation is said to decrease. Krull (1987, 1989) compared CV syllables from Swedish spontaneous speech with corresponding syllables in read speech. Results suggested that there is more coarticulation in spontaneous speech, supporting Lindblom's hypothesis. The further suggestion was made that this is because syllables are shorter here than in read speech, i.e. there is less time to reach the target, hence more coarticulation. However, using other measures, Hertrich and Ackermann (1995) have found that while perseverative vowel-to-vowel coarticulation is decreased in slow speech, anticipatory coarticulation actually increases for 75 per cent of their subjects. We must therefore accept Krull's results with the understanding that they may not tell the whole story.

These studies could be described as purely phonetic, but there is increasing evidence that at least some coarticulatory effects are part of the language plan rather than a simple result of articulator inertia (Whalen, 1990). This lends credence to the idea (which also forms part of the H&H theory) that in every speech act there is a fine balance between the natural tendency of the vocal tract to under-articulate and the need to maintain adequate communication.

The idea that variation can exist up to but not including the point where contrast is lost (except in cases of neutralization) is not new. It can be traced at least to Trubetzkoy (1969 [1939]), who observes (p. 73), for example, that in German there is much room for different pronunciations of /r/, since it needs to be distinguished only from /l/. In Czech, however, pronunciations are more constrained, since /r/ must contrast with both /l/ and the retroflex sibilant /zˌ/. Manuel (1987) suggests, in a similar vein, that languages with small vowel inventories allow greater variation for a given vowel than languages with larger inventories.

### Palatographic studies

Electropalatography (EPG) offers a unique opportunity to look at casual speech processes because it allows us to measure the degree of contact between the tongue dorsum and the roof of the mouth.

Typical electropalatograms (EPGms) of careful speech show exactly what might be predicted from an IPA chart. For example for English [d], one sees a complete closure at the alveolar ridge and considerable contact between the sides of the tongue and the edge of the palate near the molars (figure 4.1a). The molar contact, while not a typical part of a phonetic description, is a normal consequence of a raised tongue body and is seen for canonic high vowels as well.

A striking feature of EPGms of most casual speech is that there is less contact, especially molar contact, than that found in citation forms (Hardcastle, personal communication), reflecting less extreme movement of the tongue. As has been surmised from acoustic displays, (Lindblom, 1963, 1964), it seems that the space used for articulation decreases when sounds are strung together, presumably so as to maximize the efficiency of the gestures. One might compare the tongue to a player of a racquet sport who tries to remain as near the centre of the court as possible, in order to minimize the distance travelled to intercept the next volley. In Lindblom's words, 'Unconstrained, a motor system tends to default to a low-cost form of behaviour' (1990: 413). In casual speech, even given linguistic constraints, the tongue only rarely achieves the most peripheral positions. Of course, there is a wide range of divergence from 'most peripheral', some of which, though visible on an EPG, is not detectable by ear. Lindblom uses this notion as a partial explanation of vowel reduction in English, but even languages which do not show a marked tendency of movement towards schwa in unstressed syllables show reduced tongue-palate contact in casual speech.

A large study of connected speech processes (called CSPs by the Cambridge group) using EPG was done at the University of Cambridge, results of which appeared in a series of articles over a decade (Nolan, 1986; Barry, 1984, 1985, 1991; Wright, 1986; Kerswill, 1985; Kerswill and Wright, 1989; Nolan and Kerswill, 1990; Nolan and Cobb, 1994). Much of the research was aimed at describing the accent used by natives of Cambridge, and results were often congruent with those reported in chapter 2 of this book: CSPs fell into categories such as deletion, weakening, assimilation, and reduction. Their work emphasized that most CSPs produce a continuum rather than a binary output: if a process suggests that $a \to b$, we often find, phonetically, cases of $a$, $b$, and a rainbow of intermediate stages, some of which cannot be detected by ear. They suggest that accents of the same language can potentially be differentiated by finding their locations on such continua, though there is also idiosyncratic variation and variation among speakers of a particular accent.

In addition, the motivations behind the CSPs are heterogeneous, ranging from articulatory to grammatical. The Cambridge studies showed that attention was a determinant of reduction: at a rate where reduction would be predicted, it could be eliminated by focusing on articulation. (A study I carried out (Shockey, 1987) bears this out: at their fastest rate, my subjects found it possible to articulate all target segments in a reduction-prone sentence if they concentrated on articulating carefully.) In addition, they found that rate and style contributed to reduction. Wright (1986) looked at alveolar place assimilation, l-vocalization, palatalization, and t-glottalling in a data set where three subjects read reduction-prone sentences at slow, normal, and fast rates. She concluded that l-vocalization and palatalization were relatively insensitive to rate while the others showed greater frequency at faster rates. She adds that while t-glottalling diminishes in fast speech, it is largely because the 't' undergoes other processes such as deletion or complete assimilation. She concludes that t-glottalling is not in itself rate sensitive, but that it interacts with other processes in a rate sensitive manner. Alveolar assimilation was especially rate-sensitive, with much higher rates of complete assimilation at greater speeds.

The Cambridge group emphasize that, while CSPs may appear natural, they are language-specific and even accent-specific and hence cannot be mechanical effects, a point introduced here in chapter 1.

Papers on the importance of non-binary output to phonological theory (Nolan, 1992, Holst and Nolan, 1995a, 1995b) and on modelling assimilation (Nolan and Holst, 1996) have also come out of this work.

The majority of the work just described used 'laboratory speech' – read lists of words and/or phrases containing sequences likely to reduce. Nolan and Kerswill (1990) used the Map Task, a clever technique (see Brown et al., 1984 and Anderson et al., 1991) in which mapped landmarks with desirable phonological shapes are discussed by two people on opposite sides of a screen. The lack of visual cues and the fact that the maps which the two parties are looking at are somewhat different causes much repetition of the landmark names under a variety of discourse conditions, resulting in a usable corpus of unselfconsciously-produced data.

Shockey (1991) used EPG to look at unscripted casual speech. One subject wearing an electropalate and a friend were asked to sit in a sound-treated room and converse naturally about whatever occurred to them. The experimenter, outside the booth, waited for the subjects to become immersed in conversation, then collected three-second extracts of both acoustic and EPG data at random intervals. The excerpts were then transcribed and examined for casual speech effects, with special attention to /t, d, n, l, s/ and /z/. All alveolars showed a tendency towards reduced stricture intervocalically. /d/ was normally fully articulated after /l/ and /z/, especially when the next word began with a vowel, and was normally not present in the environment n_C. /t/ is not realized in the same environment.

The openness of some fricatives was remarkable. In some cases, it seemed that it would be hard to create turbulence in such an open channel, and, in fact, there was a highly reduced noise level acoustically. Figure 4.1 shows illustrations of citation-form and casual alveolar consonants, in both citation form and casual speech. Each frame (similar to frames in a cinefilm) shows 10 milliseconds of speech. The rounded top represents the front of the palate, beginning from just behind the teeth. The squared-off bottom represents the back of the hard palate (the plastic artificial palate cannot extend backwards over the soft palate as it interferes with movement and causes discomfort). The symbol '0' shows where the tongue is touching the roof of the mouth.

Traces nearly identical in their lack of molar contact can be found in Italian (Shockey and Farnetani, 1992) and French (Shockey, work in progress) casual tokens, suggesting that the lowered tongue position is generally characteristic of spontaneous speech.

Docherty and Fraser (1993: 17), based on a study of read speech containing a high percentage of alveolar and palato-alveolar

```
    47          48          49          50          51          52
  00000.      000000      000000      000000      000000      000000
 00000000    00000000    00000000    00000000    00000000    00000000
 00000.00    00000000    00000000    00000000    00000000    00000000
 0......0    00.....0    00.....0    00.....0    00.....0    00.....0
 0......0    0......0    0......0    0......0    0......0    0......0
 .......     ......0     0......0    0......0    0......0    0......0
 0......0    0......0    0......0    0......0    0......0    0......0
 00....00    00....00    00....00    00....00    00....00    00....00
```

(a) first [d] from lab speech utterance [dida]

```
    210         211         212         213
  000000      000000      000000      00..0.
 00000000    00000000    000..000    00....00
 00....00    00....00    00....00    00.....0
 0......0    0......0    0......0    0......0
 0......0    0......0    0......0    0......0
 0......0    0......0    0......0    0......0
 0......0    0......0    0......0    0......0
 000...00    000...00    00....00    00....00
```

(b) first [d] from casual speech 'speeded'

```
    220         221         222         223
  00..0.      000.0.      000.0.      00....
 000....0    0000.000    00.....0    0.......
 0......0    0......0    0.......    0.......
 ........    ........    ........    ........
 ........    ........    ........    ........
 ........    ........    ........    ........
 ........    ........    ........    ........
 00.....0    .......0    .......0    .......0
```

(c) second [d] from casual speech 'speeded'

```
    91          92          93          94
  ......      0.....      0.....      ......
 0.......    00.....0    0......0    0......0
 0......0    0......0    0......0    0.......
 0.......    0.......    0.......    0.......
 ........    ........    ........    ........
 ........    ........    ........    ........
 ........    ........    .......0    .......0
 .......0    00.....0    00.....0    00.....0
```

(d) [d] from casual speech 'already'

*Figure 4.1*  Citation-form and casual alveolar consonants in both citation form and casual speech
(a) citation form [d]. This token is much longer than the others, as well as showing more tongue–palate contact.
(b) first [d] in connected speech word 'speeded' (similar to citation form).
(c) second [d] in 'speeded'. Note lack of molar contact.
(d) very open [d] from 'already'. Note general lack of contact.

consonants, comment, '[EPG] data calls into question the validity of using stricture-based definitions for manner-of-articulation categories at all.' They point out that while stricture categories are adequate for description of citation-form speech, they can be confusing when they are applied to connected speech, in which strictures are more open than expected.

### 4.1.2 Production/Perception studies of particular processes

#### Vowel devoicing

It will be remembered that vowel devoicing was found to occur in casual speech forms such as [pə̥'tɛɪtəʊ] and [tə̥'kip].

Rodgers (1999) cites two possible causes of vowel devoicing. The first from Ohala (1975) is that high oral air pressure delays the onset of voicing (i.e., there is a time lapse while subglottal pressure builds up sufficiently to cause phonation). The second from Beckman (1996) is simply that the vocalic gesture assimilates to the voicelessness of surrounding segments. Ohala's hypothesis favours devoicing in high vowels, as the high tongue position creates a small oral cavity and hence high pressure. Rodgers cites Jaeger (1978), who looked at 30 languages with vowel devoicing and found that low vowels do not devoice. Greenberg (1969) confirms that no vowel that is voiceless is lower than schwa.

Using air pressure as a predictor, Rodgers hypothesized that the following factors are conducive to vowel devoicing:

1 place of articulation: vowels between two voiceless velars will devoice more than those between two alveolars because the smaller the oral cavity, the greater the back pressure on the vocal folds;
2 lack of stress, since unstressed vowels have lower air pressure than stressed ones;
3 vowel height, as suggested above;
4 rounding, since rounding slows transglottal pressure drop;
5 voiceless stop or fricative in coda.

Texts containing appropriate sequences were constructed and read fluently by native speakers of SSB. Results did not support hypothesis 1: instead, there was greater devoicing after alveolars. This may be because an unstressed vowel after an alveolar obstruent and especially between two of them is essentially identical to the high central [ɨ], which brings it in the domain of hypothesis 3. Hypotheses 2–4 were supported, with stress and vowel height being more influential than rounding. Hypothesis 5 was not supported, probably because final obstruents are not significantly voiced in English. An interesting additional finding was that light syllables (with a short vowel and one final consonant) devoice more than heavy syllables: *antic* was relatively more voiceless than *artist*.

Rodgers also finds that rhythm is important for devoicing: the greater number of syllables in a foot, the greater the devoicing, and the nearer an unstressed syllable is to a stress, the more it will devoice.

In further work on articulatory speech synthesis, Rodgers also backs up Beckman's theory of laryngeal assimilation. He concludes that air pressure and laryngeal inertia interact in producing voiceless vowels in connected speech.

### Schwa incorporation

Several researchers have looked at aspects of schwa incorporation. Two early studies suggest that segments into which schwa is incorporated are longer than similar sounds in which schwa does not play a part. First, Price (1980) did a perceptual study in which she varied duration and amplitude in the /r/ portion of naturally-spoken utterances of 'parade' and 'prayed'. Duration had a decisive effect on listener judgements for both words, but the effect of amplitude was negligible except in ambiguous situations. In a further experiment, she varied the duration of aspiration in words 'polite' and 'plight'. Increasing the duration of voicing of /l/ effectively switched judgements from 'plight' to 'polite'. She concluded that (1) duration is a more effective cue to sonority than is amplitude, (2) amplitude may play a role when duration is ambiguous, (3) when duration is manipulated, voiced segments tend to be more sonorant than hiss-excited segments, which in turn appear more sonorant than silence.

In the second study Roach, Sergeant and Miller (1992) found a clear difference (p < 0.001 in all pairs) in duration between syllabic and non-syllabic [r] as found in a large labelled database. They found that this difference could also be used as a cue for syllabic [l] in automatic speech recognition, but that it was not was not so effective for syllabic [n].

But a different conclusion was reached by Fokes and Bond (1993), who investigated the difference between 'real' (underlying) and 'created' (schwa-incorporated) s + C clusters as taken from read sentences in a laboratory situation. They found that there were no consistent group patterns differentiating created clusters from real clusters, based on either absolute durations or durations calculated as proportions of sequences. The stops in created clusters were not always aspirated, and not all speakers used a longer 's' in created clusters. Instead, individual speakers used different patterns in the duration of the initial fricative, voice timing, stop closure, and the duration of the stressed vowels. From the duration measurements, it could be hypothesized that some speakers' productions of created clusters would be much easier to identify than others.

In the same study, perceptual tests suggested that there were no obvious durational cues which listeners used to distinguish created clusters from real clusters. Listeners could identify words with created clusters as derived from unstressed syllables, though the identification scores varied considerably from speaker to speaker and test token to test token. Fokes and Bond conclude that the cues for identifying created clusters as [syllabic] must be more complex than the individual differences in [s] duration, closure, voice onset time, or the duration of the stressed vowel. Perhaps a combination or interaction among the measures signals the intended word. The influence of the lexicon is strong: listeners may expect syncope for some words and not others.

Manuel (1991) reports a pilot study using transillumination which suggested that there is a gesture towards glottal closure (i.e. an attempt at voicing) in 's'port' (support) at the place one would expect a schwa. Further acoustic analysis shows that the [s] in 'sport' shows a 'labial tail' (lowering of fricative frequency as the lips approximate for the [p]), little or no aspiration at the release of the [p], and no sign of glottal closure.

Manuel (personal communication, 2002) reports that occasionally one or two weak vocal fold cycles were detectable in places where the schwa was judged auditorily to be absent. This is a persistent but little-discussed feature of casual speech: there are stages between full presence and full absence which may be visible on a spectrogram but are not reliably detectable by ear, as noted in my 1974 paper (p. 42). The same can be said of vowel + nasal + stop sequences where the vowel is nasalized and the nasal is judged not to have an acoustic presence: there is often a very short segment which can be identified as a vestigial nasal consonant (see Lovins, 1978 below). These minimal displays support the Prosodic/ Gestural Phonology notion that gestures are not, in fact, deleted, but only diminished, because if this is true, we would expect to find a range from full realization to minimum realization to nothing measurable. (As mentioned in chapter 3, the acoustic difference between deletion and radical diminution seems a philosophical rather than a scientific debate.)

In perceptual tests using synthetic speech, Manuel (1991) showed that listeners can use length of aspiration to make the sport/support distinction, especially if there is no sign of a vowel. If there is even a hint of voicing where the vowel should be, listeners heard 'support'. She concludes that listeners can make use of information which is consistent with an underlying disyllabic word to access that word, even when the vowel of the first syllable has lost its oral gesture.

Beckman (1996) identifies schwa (or short, high) vowel incorporation as a feature of many languages, but claims that whether it leads to a difference in perceived number of syllables depends on the language. In Japanese, it does not; in English, it may. Violation of phonotaxis may lead to an increased probability of the incorporating item being heard as syllabic in English: [ftɒmʐɛ] 'if Tom's there' may be heard as trisyllabic simply because [ft] is not a permissible initial cluster. Warner (1999) supports the notion that syllable structure constraints of a language can influence weighting of perceptual cues. Beckman also observes that the presence of a homophone may influence interpretation of reductions, as may suprasegmental and sociolinguistic factors.

ð-*assimilation*

Manuel (1995) finds that in [n] + [ð] sequences, the [ð] does not assimilate completely, but is simply articulated with a lowered velum and without frication. This means that in a sequence such as 'win the game', the n + ð cluster is articulated as a long nasal which begins as an alveolar and moves to a dental position. There is even some evidence (p. 462) that dentality can spread throughout the nasal. There are hence two cues for the underlying cluster: the length of the resulting nasal and the formant transitions into and out of the long nasal. Manuel suggests that the formant transitions are the major perceptual cue, though she notes that Shockey (1987) found that the length in itself can be an effective cue to the underlying cluster. In order to factor out the length feature, Manuel presented pairs such as 'I'm gonna win those today' (with assimilated ð) and 'I'm gonna win noes today' to 15 subjects, who distinguished them easily (though one might argue that the suprasegmental features of these sentences are not identical). Taken together, the results suggest that both duration and frequency of F2 are used to identify [n] + [ð] sequences. More research is needed on other such sequences involving underlying alveolars + [ð], to understand the perceptual tradeoff between duration and frequency of F2.

## Tapping

Zue and Laferriere (1979) looked at read tokens of medial /t, d/ in various environments in Am. Of 250 chosen words, half were t/d minimal pairs (e.g. latter/ladder). They remind us that 'flaps' can be made in more than one way: depending on the immediate phonetic environment, the tongue tip can make contact with the alveolar ridge in a simple up-and-down movement or in a trajectory as the tongue moves in a front-back direction. The closure can be complete or partial, and in the latter case a certain amount of turbulence can be generated. They found that flaps are longer after high front vowels than after all others and suggest that this is because if the tongue is already high, the flap gesture will overshoot, resulting in a longer closure. Occasional (10 per cent) pronunciation of intervocalic 'nt' clusters as [n] was observed, an Am. characteristic. About 18 per cent of /n/s were realized as nasalization on the previous vowel in /nt/ clusters, whereas this essentially never happened in /nd/ clusters. This tallies with our observations in chapter 2. Post-lateral /t/ was normally realized as a fully articulated [t], while a larger percentage of post-lateral /d/s were realized as flap. Zue and Laferriere assume that the /l/ was not fully articulated in these cases.

Ninety-five per cent of Zue and Laferriere's underlying /t/s and /d/s were realized as flaps. Patterson and Connine (in press), basing their conclusions on the very much larger SWITCHBOARD corpus, found a very similar percentage of flaps overall, but discovered some sub-generalizations: low-frequency words showed a lower frequency of tapping than high-frequency words, and morphologically complex words showed a lower incidence of tapping than morphologically simple words. The latter result correlates nicely with results for t-glottalling found by sociolinguists, as mentioned in chapter 2.

In Zue and Laferriere's data, there was no essential difference in flaps originating from /t/ and /d/, but sonorants preceding taps derived from /d/ tended to be longer than those before flaps derived from /t/. Both Malecot and Lloyd (1968) and Fox and Terbeek (1977) made similar observations for vowels before flaps derived from /t/ and /d/, but Turk (1992) found that vowels preceding flapped /d/s are significantly longer than vowels preceding tapped /t/s only when the vowel before the flap is unstressed (p. 127). She also suggests that dialectal/idiolectal differences play a role in lengthening before voicing phenomena.

Zue and Laferriere note that deciding whether a particular token is a flap or a short [d] is often very difficult perceptually. One might argue that a genuine [d] will show an abrupt release while a tap or flap will not, so in theory the difference can be determined acoustically. In practice, even fully articulated [d]s sometimes show little release. Based on recordings in the Wellington Corpus of Spoken New Zealand English, Holmes (1994) concluded that tapping (called T voicing in this case: /d/ apparently does not tap in this accent) is favoured between vowels of unlike stress (8 per cent were before stressed syllables), and especially disfavoured between stressed vowels. /t/ was marginally more likely to tap after short vowels than long ones. The most important linguistic factor was position in word: 'word-final /t/ is is much more likely to be voiced than morpheme-final or medial /t/', even when the phrase 'sort of', in which tapping nearly always occurs, was removed from consideration. De Jong (1998) investigated whether Am. 'flapping' could be a by-product of consonant-vowel coarticulation and the encoding of prosodic organization in the jaw movement profile, using X-ray microbeam data. He postulated that the difference between an alveolar oral stop and a tap could arise as a non-linearity in the mapping of articulatory behaviour onto acoustic output and may be merely an 'epiphenomenon' rather than a phonological process.

Results show, however, a more complex situation: tapping is voluntary – some speakers opted not to do it from time to time. There is an inconsistent relationship between prosodic structure and the occurrence of tapping, and the presence of a word boundary can but does not necessarily have an effect. Thus, the flapping rule must be couched within some sort of theoretical apparatus which allows it to relate probabilistically to the various conditions which trigger it.

> Jaw position does not differ consistently between taps and stops . . . one suspects that [the] connection between tongue body positioning in the following vowel and tap perception is, like the results for jaw positioning, due to parallel reduction effects on the consonant and on the vowel, rather than due to tongue body positioning on the vowel causing the reduction of the consonant to a tap. American English stop tapping across a word boundary can be described as a variable but quasi-categorial rule, so long as the objects of the rule's description are taken to be acoustic in nature. The results for oral kinematics are not very encouraging for a categorical rule description, in that kinematic measures generally do not exhibit quantization according to tap and [d] categories (in accord with Zue and Laferriere, above). This situation suggests that a gradient change in articulatory behaviour is giving rise to somewhat quantized acoustic results, which in turn give rise to consistent transcriptions. (de Jong, 1998)

### /l/-vocalization

Hardcastle and Barry (1985) studied some phonetic factors influencing l-vocalization, using EPG because auditory judgements of vocalization were thought to be unreliable. The assumption is, of course, that vocalized /l/ will show no alveolar contact whereas 'normal' /l/ will show contact not unlike that for [d] or [n]. They used three speakers from SE England, two from SE Australia and one from England's West Midlands. Twelve words containing /l/ after a judicious selection of vowels in coda consonant clusters were produced within carrier phrases. Results showed a general lack of vocalization for /l/ followed by an alveolar stop or sibilant. About 12 per cent of these cases showed only partial closure for the [l], this being the subset which preceded [s] or [z]. It was assumed that anticipation of the groove for these fricatives explained the lack of central closure for the laterals. l-vocalization was strongly favoured before velar and palato-alveolar consonants.

They also found that vocalization occurred more often with front vowels than back ones and postulated a perceptual cause for this fact: 'the velar component of [velarized l], manifested in the vocalized examples as a close or half-close back vowel contrasts more clearly with front vowels than back vowels, making the contribution of actual alveolar contact for the /l/ identification less important' (p. 43).

Shockey's (1991) general study of alveolars in two speakers of SSB showed a regular pattern: tongue-dorsum contact was seen when /l/ was intervocalic or following a consonant but otherwise there was no significant contact.

Borowski and Horvath (1997) asked 63 Australians in Adelaide to read wordlists and a short passage skillfully interlaced with laterals. Based on impressionistic transcriptions, they found that /l/ was always pronounced as a consonant in onset position and intervocalically (even when word-final). It also appeared consistently as a consonant within a syllable coda with no boundary marker, followed by an onset consonant (as in 'Nelson', similar to the findings reported above). In this accent, /l/ was most likely to vocalize if syllabic (bottle), but even here, a following vowel-initial word inhibited vocalization (middle of). The next most conducive environment for vocalization was in coda position after a 'long' vowel (feel, cool) and the third most conducive was in a consonant cluster after a 'short' vowel (silk, milk). (Several back vowels before /l/ were included in the experiment (e.g. old, sold, cool, school), but a correlation between vowel front/backness and vocalization was apparently not noted, unlike Hardcastle and Barry). They conclude that vocalization is related to the relative sonority of the syllabic position occupied by the /l/: the closer to the nucleus, the more likely vocalization is. They point out that the behaviour of /l/ in their accent is nearly symmetrical with that of /r/ but variable rather than categorical. /r/ is non-rhotic in most of the places where /l/ is most likely to become syllabic ('Nelson' being a counterexample).

### Nasal deletion

There has traditionally been great interest in the timing relationship between lingual, laryngeal and velar movements in connected speech. My impression is that there is agreement that normally the velum is down during nasal consonants and that there is considerable variation across languages and even across speakers of the same language in how soon the velum lowers during the previous vowel in a VN sequence. There is a gap in the literature with respect to experimental studies of nasal deletion in casual speech, but Lovins (1978) looks at the issue in American English lab speech. Her study is a response to phonologists, who have at times regarded nasal deletion as categorical:

$$V \rightarrow [+\text{nasalized}] \mathbin{/} \_\_ N \quad N \rightarrow 0 \mathbin{/} \_\_\_ C, [-\text{voice}]$$

Lovins observes that one could think of the nasal property as 'moving left' rather than actually being deleted but goes on to say that 'deletion' is, in the majority of cases, not a strictly appropriate term for what happens (in Am.). The only time the nasal is truly deleted (based on observation of spectrograms) is when a following /t/ is pronounced as glottal stop (as in [kãʔ]): in most cases, a small amount of nasal murmur remains before the voiceless stop. Its duration depends on speaker style, rate, and other variables. She grants that the nasal murmur which remains before a voiceless stop is hard to hear, which accounts for the percept that it is deleted.

She attributes the shortness of the nasal murmur to the general tendency to shorten syllable nuclei before voiceless consonants in (most languages which have been investigated, but especially) English.

## 4.2 Perception of Casual Speech

### 4.2.1 Setting the stage

Within a given language, words often take on multiple forms and the relationships (amongst) these forms are generally lawful . . . For the average listener, such variations apparently cause no great difficulty, even on first hearing a new variant of some familiar lexical item, provided that the context is appropriate. (Jusczyk in Perkell and Klatt, 1986: 13).

*Tuning in*

While listening to and interpreting relaxed, unselfconscious speech is a feat which we all perform with a high degree of accuracy every day, no one really understands how it is done. Casual speech is often produced at a relatively fast rate and uses the short cuts which are described in chapter 2: how can the perceptual system keep up with the flow of incoming information?

One traditional answer is that speech perception happens though 'normalization'. This means that the hearer factors out all the real-time-dependent variables such as rate and coarticulation, all the speaker-dependent variables such as voice type/range and head/articulator idiosyncracies, and all the place-dependent variables such as room acoustics in order to match the input with items in the mental lexicon, which are thought to be stored as careful forms.

It seems likely that aspects of normalization are learned: Jusczyk (1999: 123) has shown, for example that infants do not do well at perceiving speech in noise, and speech rate is usually drastically reduced by adults speaking to children, presumably as a result of noticing that very young children cannot deal with rapid speech. (Alternatively, they may speak slowly to children because children speak slowly to them.)

Most researchers agree that some sort of perceptual framework needs to be rapidly established at the outset of a conversational interchange in order for communication to be successful: each member of a dialogue will 'home in on' the characteristics of the other speaker immediately upon his or her speaking, and these perceptual settings will facilitate the understanding of subsequent utterances by the same speaker. Mullennix et al. (1989) have shown that word lists read aloud by random voices are much harder to identify accurately than lists read aloud by a single speaker, presumably because in the former case one cannot establish a stable perceptual basis.

'Tuning in' seems to be essential for the understanding of casual speech as well: experiments asking subjects to identify words excised from conversations (Pickett and Pollack, 1963: 64) yield very low success rates, and further cases will be presented below.

### Modelling speech perception

Casual speech has not been a major concern of speech perception theories in the twentieth century, and, indeed, most theories of speech perception appear to regard spoken language as equivalent to written language in that it is thought to be composed of a linear sequence of distinct items each of which can be recognized in turn. Any type of deviation from citation form, whether patterned or random, is regarded as noise. There are two major exceptions:

1   The Lindblom-MacNeilage H&H theory, mentioned previously, which assumes that linguistic and physical context figure prominently in establishing communication between speaker and hearer. Each act of spoken language takes into account previous discourse, acoustic conditions, and the linguistic abilities of both speaker and hearer, using the least energy necessary to get the message across. So, in a case where speaker and hearer have the same accent, have been involved in a conversation for some time, and enjoy a good acoustic environment, it is possible to 'cut corners' and use Hypo-articulation (under-articulation). But in a case where, for example, the two speakers have very different accents or there is some other factor such as noise to prevent perfect understanding, speakers will move towards more careful speech (Hyper-articulation, hence H&H). Lindblom and MacNeilage hence see carefulness as a continuum, the point on which each individual speech event takes place being determined by a variety of factors.

While this is an attractive model, it is very difficult to apply in a deterministic fashion, since our knowledge of the contribution of the many variables to the articulation of each utterance is slight. At present, it could be thought of as a *qualitative* rather than a *quantitative* model.

2   Fowler's gestural model (1985) is designed to explain both speech production and perception. It postulates that speech is composed of gestures and complexes of gestures. The limits of these are set by the nature of the vocal tract and the human perceptual system, but there is room within these limits for variation across languages. Many languages could have a voiceless velar stop gesture, for example, but the relationship among tongue movement, velum movement, and laryngeal activity can differ from language to language. These differences can in turn account for differences in coarticulation across languages. Fowler suggests that language is both produced and perceived in terms of these gestures. Consequently, there is no need for a special mapping of speech onto abstract language units such as distinctive features: speech is perceived directly.

As mentioned in chapter 3 in our discussion of Browman and Goldstein (who have a similar approach, though they regard it as phonological rather than (or as well as) phonetic), gestures can differ only in amplitude and in the amount with which they overlap with neighbouring gestures. It is thus assumed that all connected speech phenomena are explicable in terms of these two devices, and is presumably further assumed that perception of conversational speech does not differ significantly from perception of careful or formal speech, since the same gestures are used in each case.

### The word

A very popular psycholinguistic model (or family of models) of speech perception (Marslen-Wilson and Welsh, 1978; Cole and Jakimik, 1978; Cutler and Norris, 1988, Norris, 1994) assumes that the word is the basic unit of perception and that the mental lexicon is where sound and meaning are united. When this union occurs, a percept is achieved.

A person hearing a new utterance will take in enough acoustic information to recognize the first perceptual unit (sound, syllable, stress unit). A subconscious search in the mental lexicon will bring up all words beginning with this unit. These words are said to be 'in competition' for the time slot. As the time course of the phonetic information is followed and more units are perceived, words which do not match are discarded. A word is recognized when there are no other candidates ('the isolation point'). When recognition involves a grammatical unit such as a phrase or sentence, semantic and syntactic analyses become stronger as the parse progresses, so that fewer lexical items are brought up in any given position, and recognition gets faster. There are a few additional principles, such as that frequent words are easier to recognize than unusual ones and words which have been used recently are easier to recognize than words which are just being introduced into the discourse.

This theory is different from several earlier ones because it is largely automatic, i.e. it does not need a control device which compares input with stored templates to decide whether there is a good match: it simply works its way along the input until a winner is declared. An ongoing argument in the word recognition literature is to what extent phonetic information is supplemented by higher-level (syntactic, semantic) information, especially at later stages in the utterance (Cutler, 1995).

The psychological reality and primacy of the word is an essential foundation of this theory, and especially the *beginning* of the word, which is usually taken as the entry point for perceptual processing. (Counterevidence exists: see Cutler, 1995: 102–3, but highest priority is still given in the model to word-initial information.) It is perhaps no accident that most of the experimentation associated with this model has been done in what Whorf (1941) called Standard Average European languages and other languages where morphology is relatively simple and the division between words and higher-level linguistic units is relatively clear. It is arguable whether it is a good perceptual model for, say, Russian, which has a number of prefixes which can be added to verbs to change aspect (Comrie,

1987: 340; Lehiste, personal communication) such that there will be, for example, thousands of verbs beginning with 'pro', a perfective prefix. Even English has several highly productive prefixes such as 'un-'. Given a way can be found to 'fast forward' over prefixes (while at the same time noting their identity), there may still be problems for this model with languages such as Inuktitut, which has over 500 productive affixes and where the distinction between words and sentences is very vague indeed: 'Ajjiliurumajagit' means, for example 'I want to take your picture', and 'Qimuksikkuurumavunga' means 'I want to go by dogteam.' The structure of the Inuktitut lexicon is a subject far beyond the remit of this book, but it seems likely that the lexical access model hypothesized for English will be heavily tested by this language.

Another challenge to this model is presented by the perception of casual speech which, as we have seen, often has portions where acoustic information is spread over several notional segments (so that strict linearity is not observed) or is sometimes missing entirely.

### 4.2.2 Phonology in speech perception

#### Does it play a part at all?

Theories of word perception are largely proposed by psychologists, who recognize the acoustic/phonetic aspects of sound but who (*pace* those cited below) do not consider the place of phonology in speech perception. Most models suggest that phonetic sounds are mapped directly onto the lexicon, with no intermediate linguistic processing. But to a linguist, it seems reasonable to suppose that phonological rules or processes are involved both in speech production and speech perception. Frazier (1987: 262) makes the ironic observation that it is generally agreed that people perceive an unfamiliar language with reference to the phonology of their native language, but it is *not* agreed that they perceive their native language with reference to its own phonology. Frauenfelder and Lahiri (1989) stress that the phonology of the language does influence how it is perceived. For example (p. 331), speakers of English infer a following nasal consonant when they hear a nasalized vowel, while speakers of Bengali, which has phonemically nasalized vowels, do not. Cutler, Mehler, Norris and Segui (1983) suggest that English-speaking and French-speaking subjects process syllables differently. Gaskell and Marslen-Wilson (1998: 388) conclude, 'when listeners make judgments about the identity of segments embedded in continuous speech, they are operating on a highly analyzed phonological representation.'

It thus seems quite likely that phonology does play a part in speech perception: we could say that access to the lexicon is mediated by phonology: phonology gives us a variety of ways to interpret input because a given phonetic form could have come from a number of underlying phonological forms. We develop language-specific algorithms for interpretation of phonetic input which are congruent with production algorithms (phonological rules or processes).

Both Frauenfelder and Lahiri (1989) and Sotillo (1997: 53) note that there is one other basic approach to the problem of recognizing multiple realizations of the same word form: rather than a single form being stored and variants predicted/recognized by algorithm as suggested above, all variants are included in the lexicon (variation is 'pre-compiled'). Lahiri and Marslen-Wilson (1991) opine that this technique is both inelegant and unwieldy 'given the productivity of the phonological processes involved'. This theoretical bifurcation can be seen as a subset of the old 'compute or store' problem which has been discussed by computer scientists: is it easier to look up information (hence putting a load on memory) or to generate it on the spot (hence putting a load on computation)? A non-generative approach to phonology involving storage of variants (Trace/Event Theory) was discussed at the end of chapter 3 and will be discussed further below.

### Access by algorithm

Lahiri and Marslen-Wilson (1991) suggest lexical access through interpretation of underspecified phonological features (see chapter 3 for underspecification), an algorithmic process. They observe that lexical items must be represented such that they are distinct from each other, but at the same time they must be sufficiently abstract to allow for recognition of variable forms. Therefore, all English vowels will be underspecified for nasality in the lexicon, allowing both nasal and non-nasal vowels to map onto them. Some Bengali vowels will either be specified [+*nasal*], allowing for mapping of nasalized vowels which do not occur before nasals or *unspecified*, allowing for mapping of both nasalized vowels before nasals and non-nasalized vowels.

Similarly, English coronal nasals will be unspecified for place, so that the first syllable of ['pɪmbɔl] ['pɪŋkuʃn] and ['pɪnhɛd] can all be recognized as 'pin'. Marslen-Wilson, Nix and Gaskell (1995) refine this concept by noting that phonologically-allowed variants of coronals are not recognized as coronals if the following context is not present, such that abstract representation and context-sensitive phonological inference each play a part in recognition.

In allowing a degree of abstraction, this theory undoubtedly gets closer to the truth than the simple word-access machine described above, but at the expense of a strictly linear analysis. For example, speakers of Bengali will have to wait to see whether there is a nasal consonant following before assigning a nasalized vowel to the [+nasal] or [−nasal] category, so recognition of a word cannot proceed segment by segment.

### Late recognition: gating experiments

*Gating* is a technique for presentation of speech stimuli which is often used when judgements about connected speech are required. Normally, connected speech goes by so fast that hearers are not capable of determining the presence or absence of a particular segment or feature. In gating, one truncates all but a small amount of the beginning of an utterance, then re-introduces the deleted material in small increments ('gates') until the entire utterance is heard. This yields a continuum of stimuli with ever greater duration and hence ever greater information. When gated speech is played to subjects and they are asked to make a judgement about what they hear, the development of a sound/word/sentence percept can be tracked.

Word recognition often occurs later than the simple word-recognition theory would predict. Grosjean (1980), for example, discovered that gated words taken from the speech stream were recognized very poorly and many monosyllabic words were not totally accepted until after their completion. Luce (1986) agrees that many short words are not accepted until the following word is known and concludes that it is virtually impossible to recognize a word in fluent speech without first having heard the entire word as well as a portion of the next word. Grosjean (1985) suggested that the recognition process is sequential but not always in synchrony with the acoustic-phonetic stream (though his own futher experiments showed this to be inaccurate).

Bard, Shillcock and Altmann (1988) presented sentences gated in words to their subjects. Although the majority of recognition outcomes (69 per cent) yielded success in the word's first presentation with prior context only, 19 per cent of all outcomes and 21 per cent of all successful outcomes were late recognitions.

These late recognitions were not merely an artefact of the interruption of word-final coarticulation. Approximately 35 per cent of them were identified not at the presentation of the next word, but later still. The mean number of subsequent words needed for late identification was closer to two than one (M = 1.69, SD = 1.32).

Their results suggested that longer words (as measured in milliseconds), content words, and words farther from the beginning of an utterance were more likely to be recognized on their first presentation. Short words near the end of an utterance, where the opportunity for late recognition was limited, were more likely to be recognized late or not at all.

## My experiments

### EXPERIMENT 1

How casual speech is interpreted has been one of my ongoing research questions. In an early experiment (Shockey and Watkins, 1995), I recorded and gated a sentence containing two notable divergences from careful pronunciation. The sentence was 'The screen play didn't resemble the book at all', pronounced as follows:

[ðə'skɹĩmplɛɪdɪ<sup>d</sup>n̩ɹɪzɛ̃mbɬðə'bʊkət'ɔɬ]

The 'n' at the end of 'screen' was pronounced 'm' (so the word was, phonetically, 'scream') and the word 'didn't' was pronounced [dɪᵈn̩], where the second 'd' was a passing, short closure before a nasal release and the final 't' did not appear at all. The gates began in the middle of the word 'screen' and were of approximately 50 msec. rather than being entire words.

At first, all subjects heard 'screen' as 'scream' which is altogether unsurprising, as that is what was said. As soon as the conditioning factor for the n → m assimilation appears, however, some subjects immediately shift from 'scream' to 'screen' without taking into account the identity of the following word. These 'hair trigger' subjects are clearly working in a phonological mode: their phonological process which assimilates 'n' to 'm' before a labial 'works in reverse' when the labial is revealed, as suggested by Gaskell and Marslen-Wilson (1998). This seems good evidence of an *active* phonology which is not simply facilitating matches with lexical forms but which is throwing up alternative interpretations whenever they become possible.

One would predict that the strategy described above could prove errorful in the case where a 'm' + 'p' sequence represents only itself. In another experiment where the intended lexical item was 'scream' rather than 'screen' but the following environment was again a 'p' ('The scream play was part of Primal Therapy'), it was discovered that some subjects indeed made the 'm' to 'n' reversal on phonetic evidence and had to reverse their decision later in the sentence.

In experiment 1, other subjects waited until the end of the word 'play' to institute the reversal of 'm' to 'n' but most had achieved the reversal by the beginning of 'didn't'. Subjects who wait longer and gather more corroborating evidence from lexical identity and/or syntactic structures are clearly using a more global strategy.

With the word 'didn't' it is apparent that the results reflect such a global judgement: the word is much more highly-reduced than 'screen' and the time span over which it is recognized is much greater. Three subjects did not identify the word correctly until after the word 'book,' and only one subject recognized the word within its own time span. Interestingly, the subjects who did not arrive at a correct interpretation of the entire sentence were those who did not apply the global technique: they arrived at an incorrect interpretation early on and did not update their guess based on subsequent information.

Results of this experiment thus suggested that there is a class of very simple phonological processes which can be 'reversed' locally, but that processes which seriously alter the structure of a word need to be resolved using a larger context.

## EXPERIMENT 2

Experiment 1 was criticized on two grounds: (1) the sentence used was not a sentence taken from natural conversation, hence results yet again reflected perception of 'lab speech'; and (2) the speaker in this case had an American accent, but the subjects were users of British English. Conversational processes might be different for the two varieties, and if so this would interfere with identification of the sentence by British subjects.

With these in mind, I chose a sentence from a recorded monologue taken from a native speaker of Standard Southern British, gated it using 50 msec. gates from very near the beginning, and presented the result, interspersed with suitable pauses, to a new group of users of Southern British.

The sentence was 'So it was quite good fun, actually, on the wedding, though.' It was pronounced:

[sʷɪʷəʷsˈkwaɪʔɡʊd̥fʌnæʧʊwɪɒnn̩əˈwɛdɨ̞ŋd̥θʉ]

This sentence was chosen for three main reasons: (1) it was one of the few from the recordings of connected speech I had collected which seemed clearly understandable out of context, (2) it contained familiar casual speech reductions, presumably having as a basis:

[səʊɪtwəzˈkwaɪtɡʊdfʌnækʃʊəliɒnðəˈwɛdɨ̞ŋðəʊ]

and (3) it had a slightly unusual construction and the major information came quite late in the sentence. This meant that the well-known phenomenon of words being more predictable as the sentence unfolds was minimized.

Despite the match between accent of speaker and hearer, scores on perception of the sentence were not perfect: mistakes took place at the very-much-reduced beginning of the sentence, as seen below. Here are examples of answer sequences from non-linguists:

*Subject A*
1   i
2   pee
3   pquo
4   pisquoi
5   pisquoi
6   pisquoit
7   ?
8   pisquoifana
9   pisquoifanat
10  pisquoifanactually
11  etc. along the same lines . . .
20  He's quite good fun, actually, on the wedding day.

*Subject B*
1   tu
2   tut
3   uka
4   uzka
5   she's quite
6   she's quite a
7   she's quite a fun
8   she's quite a fun ac
9   she's quite good fun, ac
10  so it was quite good fun, actually . . .

Following is an example of an answer sheet from a subject who also was a phonetician and could use phonetic transcription to reflect the bits which were not yet understood:

1   tsu
2   tsut
3   tsukɒ
4   tsuzkɒ
5   she's quite

6    she's quite a
7    she's quite a fun
9    she's quite good fun ac . . .
10   so it was quite good fun, actually on

The major feature of these responses is disorientation until gate 10 (20, the last gate, for subject A), when the correct response suddenly appears and in a way which seems only indirectly related to earlier responses.

EXPERIMENT 3
I thought that my subjects might be limited in their responses by the spelling system of English, so constructed the following paradigm: the listener first hears a gated utterance, then repeats it, then writes it. My line of reasoning was that even if they could not use phonetic transcription, the subjects could repeat the input accurately, and I could transcribe it phonetically, thus getting a clearer insight into how the percept was developing.

For this task, a short sentence was used 'And they arrived on the Friday night.' It was produced as part of a spontaneous monologue by a speaker of Standard Southern British, isolated, and gated from the beginning. A reasonably close phonetic transcription is:

n̪ːɛɪɚaɪvdɒn̪ːəˈfɹaɪdɪˈnaɪʔt

In this sentence 'and' is reduced to a long dental nasal, 'and they' shows ð-assimilation, the [əɹ] sequence in 'arrived' is realized as [ɚ], and 'on the' is realized with ð-assimilation. Much of the reduction is at the beginning of the sentence, which makes the task harder.

Subjects, in fact, found the whole experience difficult (even though many of them were colleagues in linguistics), and nearly everyone forgot to either speak or write in one instance. With hindsight, I think the task is too difficult, and future experiments should ask for either repetition or writing, not both. It is also not clear that the spoken response adds anything to what can be gleaned from the orthographic version, even though they are often different.

There were ten gates in all. Table 4.1 shows selected results from five of them.

*Table 4.1*   Listeners' transcriptions of gated utterances

| Gate no. | My transcription | They said | Their transcription |
|---|---|---|---|
| 1 | [n̩ʔ] | n̩n | n |
|  |  | m | um |
|  |  | mɔbm | mb |
|  |  | ɦmʔ | — |
|  |  | m | m |
|  |  | ʕn | n |
|  |  | ɲjə | na |
|  |  | ʔə̃ŋʔ | un |
| 4 | n̩:ɛɪə | nɛʔ | nek |
|  |  | mɛ | mare |
|  |  | əmɛ̯ʔ | uhmay |
|  |  | m:ɛɪ | mayb |
|  |  | nɛæʊ | now |
| 6 | n̩:ɛɪɚaɛ | nɛɹə | neero |
|  |  | mɛɹæ | mare I |
|  |  | fɹəmðɛɹɑ | from there I |
|  |  | naʊɹaɪʔ | now ri |
|  |  | m:ɛɹə | mara |
|  |  | m:ɛɪɹaɪ | mayro |
| 8 | n̩:ɛɪɚaɪvd | nɛɹav | neero |
|  |  | mɛɹaɪ | mare I |
|  |  | ðɛɹaɪv | they arrive |
|  |  | mɛɪaɹɹaɪ̯t | may I write |
|  |  | miwɑɪ | may why |
|  |  | wənɛɪɚaɪvd | when they arrived |
| 9 | n̩:ɛɪɚaɪvdɒn | nɛɪɚaɪvtʰ | neerived |
|  |  | wənðɛɪɚaɪvdɒn | when they arrived on |
|  |  | əndðɛɪɚaɪvdɒn | and they arrived on |
|  |  | mɛɹiɚaɪvdɒn | Mary arrived on |
|  |  | mɛɪɚaɪvdɒn | May arrived on |

At Gate 10, there were 3 main interpretations:

(a)   And they arrived on the Friday night     40 per cent
(b)   May arrived on the Friday night           27 per cent
(c)   When they arrived on the Friday night   20 per cent

The major causes of the misinterpretations were (1) wrong beginning, (2) inattention to suprasegmentals/assimilation and (3) incorrect choice of phonological expansion.

The first of these causes bears out the claim that beginnings of
utterances are especially important. Most of the people who arrived
at interpretation (a) heard a labial section at the beginning of the
utterance and stuck to this interpretation throughout.

The second problem prevented listeners from hearing 'and they'
at the beginning of the sentence, since the 'and th . . .' part was
encoded in the long dental [n].

Interpretation (c) was also related to the perceived labiality at
the beginning of the utterance, but rather than interpret it as [m]
(and probably because of the exceptional length of the first nasal),
what they took to be a labialized nasal was interpreted as the word
'when'. This again demonstrates an active use of phonology to
reinvent the probable source of the reduction, similar to the situation described in the erroneous 'm + p' interpretations above.

WORD RECOGNITION?

It is not surprising that some aspects of these results are incom-
patible with a strict word-recognition framework: since there were
no complete words at the beginning, the subjects did not show a tendency to recognize the input as words until well into the utterance.

The phonological changes Gaskell and Marslen-Wilson deal
with in their papers are minimal – place of articulation for stops,
nasalization for vowels – so the words they were investigating were
only mildly different from the full lexical entry (and the same can
be said for Cutler, 1998, where she lists phonological reductions
which will not create difficulties for word recognition). A distinction must be made between these minor changes in pronunciation
and major structural changes such as seen in 'and they' in the

present experimental sentence: the phonetic output represents words, but not in a way which allows a straightforward interpretation. These naturally offer a much greater challenge to perception.

Situations such as the example shown below, where a subject finds a word, changes his mind, and goes back to a non-word, were also found.

1   n
2   ne
3   nek
4   nek
5   neer
6   neero
7   neer eye
8   neerive
9   neerived
10   and they arrived on the . . .

One might conclude that though there may be a preference for understanding utterances word by word and that this is the un-marked strategy when listening to clear speech, perceivers of casual speech seem quite comfortable with building up an acoustic sketch as the utterance is produced, the details of which are filled in when enough information becomes available, exactly as suggested by Brown (p. 4) in 1977. Bard (2001, personal communication) and Shillcock, Bard and Spensley (1988) interpret this perceptual strat-egy as one of finding the best pathway through a set of alternative hypotheses which are set up as soon as the input begins, similar to the 'chart parsing' or 'lattice' techniques used in speech recognition by computer (e.g. Thompson, 1991). But the striking change at gate 9 or 10 between 'interpretation as gibberish' and 'sensible interpretation' suggests to me that no viable hypotheses were actu-ally being made at the beginning of the utterance. (Bard claims that the hypotheses have been in place all along, but are not consciously accessible. Whether this can be true of the type of sentence used in experiments 2 and 3 is an empirical question.) To all appearances, rather than having been perceived word by word, the whole sentence suddenly comes into focus. The results thus encourage us to consider a model where interpretation of a whole utterance is not possible until one gets enough distance from it to be able to see how the parts fit together, i.e. a gestalt pattern perception.

Taking the many complex cues in our sentence (And they arrived . . . ) into account, one can easily see why a significant span of speech must be taken in before interpretation can be accurate. For example, the initial nasal is long, which could simply mean that the speech is slow. We need to get more information about the rate and rhythm of the utterance before it becomes obvious that the [n:] is relatively longer than a normal initial [n]. By the time we can make this judgement, we may also be able to detect that the initial nasal is dental rather than the expected alveolar. This, too, will be difficult to judge at the absolute onset of the utterance: we must home in on the speaker's articulatory space.

Psycholinguists accept that suprasegmental aspects of speech are important for perception (see Cutler, Dahan and van Donselaar, 1997 for a review) and Davis (2000) points out that short words (such as 'cap') extracted from longer words ('captain') are recognizably different in temporal structure from the same short words said on their own (cf. Lehiste, 1972; Port, 1981). However, little has been made of the fact that suprasegmental features such as timing and intonation are often preserved when segmental information is reduced and that this may help to account for the very high intelligibility of reduced speech.

### 4.2.3   Other theories

Other psycholinguistic theories offer potentially fruitful approaches to understanding perception of casual speech.

#### *Warren, Fraser*

Richard Warren is best known for his work on phonemic restoration (Warren, 1970; Warren and Obusek, 1971) in which he showed that when a cough or noise is substituted for a speech sound, listeners not only 'hear' the sound which was deleted, but have no idea where in the utterance the extraneous noise occurred. His work reflects a general interest in speech and music perception, and especially in how very fast sequences of different sounds can be heard accurately. While most theories of speech perception assume that speech is understood in the order it is produced, Warren has shown that perceivers can accurately report the presence of, say, a beep, a burst of white noise, and a click in rapid succession without being able to report accurately the order in which they occur. Hearers can thus report that the sounds were there, but not necessarily in what order. This may be a useful technique in the speech domain when perceiving sequences such as [kãʔ] ('can't'), where the original order of elements is changed.

Working in a phonemic restoration framework, Warren also showed that listeners can defer the restoration of an ambiguous word fragment in a sentence for several words, until enough context is given to allow for interpretation. 'The integration of degraded or reduced acoustic information permits comprehension of sentences when many of the cues necessary to identify a word heard in isolation are lacking' (Warren, 1999: 185). Warren's explanation of this is that holistic perception is active: no interpretation of input is achieved until an accumulation of cues allows one to suddenly understand the entire pattern (Sherman, 1971 cited in Warren, 1999). Supporting evidence comes from reports of railroad telegraphers (Bryan and Harter, 1897, 1899, reported in Warren, 1999: 184) who usually delayed several words before transcribing the ongoing message. 'Skilled storage', as he terms it, has been observed in other domains such as typing and reading aloud. As supporting evidence, he cites Daneman and Merikle (1996), who convincingly argue that measures that tax the combined processing and storage resources of working memory are better predictors of language comprehension than are measures that tax only storage.

Fraser (1992), basing her arguments on phenomenological philosophy, makes a congruent claim, i.e. that linguists are mistaken about what is Objectified by perceivers of speech: phonemes and even words may not be isolable until the entire utterance in which they are contained is understood. Words are accessible through meaning rather than vice versa.

## Massaro and FLMP

Massaro (1987) proposed a model which could be said (though not overtly by Massaro) to function holistically in the sense indicated by Warren. The Fuzzy Logical Model of Perception (FLMP) assumes that input is processed in terms of perceptual features (which are not necessarily the distinctive features proposed in phonology) and that a percept is achieved via the values of these features. A particular percept is not linked to a single feature configuration, which allows for compensatory effects. It has been shown that stress in English, for example, may be cued by a combination of change in fundamental frequency, change in duration, change in amplitude, and change in the speech spectrum (e.g. in vowel formant values). A percept of stress may be achieved by a little bit of each of these, a moderate amount of any two of these, or a lot of one. Massaro's model allows for tradeoffs of this sort as well as tradeoffs involving different sensory modes, principally hearing and vision. The aspect of this model which interests us here is that it can build up a profile of the input without making any definite decisions until necessary, just as our subjects seem to be doing in the perception of casual speech.

## Hawkins, Smith and Polysp

Hawkins and Smith (2001) have outlined a model (Polysp) which takes into account that decisions about many linguistic constructs require considerable context. They emphasize that speech perception involves relative rather than absolute decisions and come out against 'short-domainism' (p. 101). They note that 'knowing about words and larger structures makes it easier to interpret allophonic detail and *vice versa.*' Perceptual cohesion (that which makes speech natural-sounding and interpretable) is rooted in the sensory signal, but relies on knowledge. While approaching speech perception from experiments based only marginally on the perception of casual speech, Hawkins and Smith also conclude that 'understanding linguistic meaning appears to be very much dependent on the "Gestalt" conveyed by the whole signal rather than on the gradual accumulation of information from a sequence of quasi-independent cues' (p. 112).

### Access using traces: something completely different?

In chapter 3, we reported that one way to deal with casual speech phonology is to assume that traces are stored in the mental lexicon each time a word is heard. These traces will retain indexical information such as the speaker and the social milieu in which the word was uttered. Traces can be equally well used for speech recognition: every time a word which matches a trace in the lexicon is heard, the trace is activated. If it is adequately stimulated, the result will be a percept of the word associated with the trace, accompanied by its meaning. This is a passive model of language perception, as it relies on activation rather than rule application. It has its intellectual heritage in the Parallel Distributed Processor (PDP) model described below: the tokens acquired through day-to-day social interaction serve as the training phase and a brand new token brings about the testing phase, when it is assumed that the new material will stimulate a trace or a group of traces in the lexicon, consequently 'outputting' a percept.

In this model, variation is not represented through phonological rules or processes, but is present within lexical items themselves: a variant has the same relationship to the semantic part of the entry as the citation form, which might be thought of as 'first among equals'.

A model of this sort was tested by Gaskell, Hare and Marslen-Wilson (1995), using a Parallel Distributed Processor ('neural net'). This is a computer-based device which can 'learn' to map inputs into outputs. Say, for example, you wanted the PDP to output 'two' whenever 'deux' is input. You specify 'two' as the correct output, train it on multiple tokens of 'deux', and then test it with a new token of 'deux'. If it outputs the wrong thing, you correct it, and it changes its internal values in accordance with your correction. This is the sense in which 'learning' is used here. Note that the relationship between the input and output of this device is completely arbitrary: if I wanted the output '§' to occur when the input is 'phlogiston', the device would comply as long as I trained it properly.

A multi-layered PDP system has been constructed by McClelland and Elman (1986), each layer representing a level of linguistic representation (features, phonemes, words) and programmed to interact with other levels. These researchers claim that the resulting complex system (TRACE) shares features with human speech perception in being able to map acoustic input into words and in the kinds of mistakes which it makes.

Gaskell, Hare, and Marslen-Wilson trained a PDP to match a citation form on one hand with place-assimilated forms on the other (so, for example, 'screen' will be the output associated with 'screem', 'screeng' or 'screen'). 'Feature bundles' were used instead of phonetic symbols in order to reduce the arbitrariness of the mapping (so that, e.g. [m] and [n] were identical save one feature) and to look at the question of underspecification (which will not be pursued here). Results indicated that the PDP could learn that the response 'screen' could come from the mentioned set of similar-but-not-identical stimuli.

In a second experiment, phonological variants were input along with the environments which condition them, so the training data included material like 'screen play', 'screen test', 'screem play', 'screeng colour'. Again, the citation forms were given as the correct output. The PDP showed signs of learning that non-coronal segments could be mapped into coronal representations, but also made mistakes, as do humans. While one is ill-advised to accept that humans and PDPs work along the same lines, we can tentatively conclude that if PDPs can make generalizations of this sort, it is very likely that humans can, too.

Gaskell and Marslen-Wilson advocate an algorithmic approach which works on underlying phonological principles, but these experiments suggest only that many-to-one mappings are possible. If a lexical item is represented in the mind by a variety of traces with different pronunciations one of them being the citation form, the same end is achieved as when active phonological processes are in operation, but perception of a reduced form is passive rather than algorithmic: if a trace is sufficiently stimulated, a percept will occur. They admit (p. 435) that the connectionist (PDP) approach uses a single mapping process so that algorithmic activities are only indirectly represented.

A possible difficulty with this approach is that words are often phonetically vestigial in casual speech to the extent that they cannot contribute much to a lexical entry. The 'and' described in experiment 3 is realized only as a nasal consonant, and part of the information in this consonant is about place of articulation of the first sound in the following word. It may be that some sequences of words will be represented in their entirety in the trace lexicon, so that 'and they' can be a single entry.

## 4.3   Summary

Before the middle of the twentieth century, most work on English pronunciation was aimed at specifying the correct way to articulate standard citation forms. Exceptions to this were found in sociolinguistics, but comments about casual forms were buried in treatises in which the focus was on other matters. By the end of the century, interest had grown considerably, largely under pressure of increased efforts towards recognition of speech by computer (see chapter 5). It is still fair to say, however, that the study of casual speech pronunciation is underrepresented in the literature. Wells' *Accents of English* (1982) contains much useful information, but is not primarily aimed at the description of casual speech. In-depth impressionistic studies of several standard varieties (SSB., Am., Australian) have been made, but accurate, up-to-date descriptions of nonstandard varieties are extremely rare. The increased use of labelled databases will almost certainly make studies which profile the various realizations of citation forms in casual speech easier to do and therefore more frequent.

Embarking on an experimental study of casual speech production is intimidating because variables are normally not controllable and one can never predict the number of tokens of a particular process one is going to elicit, which in turn makes the application of statistical measures difficult or impossible. Both production and perception studies of tapping, t/d deletion, glottalling, l-vocalization, and many other casual speech features have, however, been done, and a patchy picture is beginning to build up about how these function in some accents of English.

Experimental studies of perception of casual speech are on the increase, though most work done by psycholinguists to date has dealt only with a few minor processes such as consonant assimilation. Preliminary results strongly suggest that phonology actively mediates between phonetic input and lexical entries in English. Phonology is not the only answer, however: holistic perception involving other information seems to be in operation in perceiving highly reduced speech.

Skoyles (2001) makes the amusing observation that speech perception theories fall into two categories: Reading and Soup. The Reading paradigm assumes that speech is processed linearly, an item (whatever these may be) at a time until a percept is achieved. Chapter 4 examines a theory of this sort and concludes that it has difficulty in accounting for the perception of casual speech sentences containing familiar reductions. The Soup paradigm assumes that information from a variety of sources is combined, not necessarily in linear or chronological order, to produce an eventual percept. This chapter suggests that the second paradigm must be taken seriously, though there is no reason to believe that it cannot function in conjunction with Reading.

# 5

# *Applications*

As suggested in earlier chapters, the fact that conversational speech processes are regular and predictable means that they can be considered part of phonology.

## 5.1  Phonology

### *5.1.1  Writ small in English, writ large in other languages*

It was argued in chapter 1 that the transition between phonetics and phonology is indeterminate, like the boundary between boiling water and the steam above it. Molecules are exchanged in both directions, and it is difficult to say whether a particular molecule at a given instant belongs to liquid or gas. The processes discussed in chapter 2 are relatively superficial, and some would say they are phonetic rather than phonological. Yet it is very noticeable that many of these processes, while relatively minor in English, form quite major parts of the phonology of other languages and language history, reflecting their status as natural processes.

Final consonant devoicing, for example, occurs in the Slavic languages, German, Dutch, Turkish, Canadian French (Archambault and Maneva, 1996) and a large number of other languages as a regular and unexceptional process. It is also found in child language, another clue to its natural status. Final devoicing can even extend to vowels in certain cases and is a regular feature of Brazilian Portuguese.

Vowel devoicing of high vowels between voiceless obstruents is a well-known feature of Japanese but also occurs in Korean (Jun and Beckman, 1994), Turkish (Jannedy, 1994) and Shanghai Chinese (Zee, 1990). It has already been mentioned in chapter 2 that vowel nasalization and nasal dropping figure prominently in the history of French and Portuguese.

L-vocalization before consonants has played a part in the history of the Romance languages e.g. Latin > Vulgar Latin *alter*, French *autre*, Spanish *otro*, Portuguese *outro*. Modern Portuguese also shows final 'l' vocalization as a living process: Spanish *mal*, Portuguese *mau*. Even when not represented in the spelling, the pronunciation of final 'l' in Portuguese is vocalic: 'hotel' [oˈtɛʊ]. In Polish, the sound which is spelled 'ł' was once a dark (velarized) [l], but in modern Polish, it is pronounced the same as [w]. While this is not exactly vocalization (given that [w] is not a vowel), it shows the same process of loss of tongue-tip contact. There are vocalic consequences: sequences spelled łu/łó or uł/ół are all pronounced [u:]. Since long vowels do not play a role in Polish, [u:] is interpreted as /wu/ or /uw/. Loss of tongue contact for 'ł' has thus brought about a reorganization of the Polish consonant system: whereas once there was a three-way contrast among ł, l, and w, there is now a two-way contrast between l and w (i.e. ł and w have coalesced) (Jassem, 2001, personal communication).

Palatalization is attributed to many languages, but it is not easy to find a language other than English in which palatalization applies only with following palatal approximants. Southern Brazilian Portuguese shows regular palatalization of /t/ and /d/ before high vowels, as in 'quente' [ˈkẽ(n)tʃi] and 'grande' [gɾɐ̃(n)dʒi]. Many other languages show a sequence k → t → tʃ, ç or ʃ before non-low vowels, Swedish (Kerstin [ˈçɛʂtɨn] and Italian cento → [ˈtʃɛnto] being obvious cases.

Lenition (weakening) is a term which crops up frequently in language descriptions. Notionally, it refers to a diminution of the energy used to pronounce an underlying phonological unit within a word in a particular linguistic environment. Lenition can have a grammatical function: in Welsh (where a typical lenition is voiceless stop → voiced stop → fricative), it gives information about word class of the word in which it applies, that of a neighbouring word or both. For example, a feminine singular noun will show lenition after the definite article: *cadair* 'chair'; *y gadair* 'the chair'. The feminine singular noun will, in turn, cause lenition in a following adjective: *merch* 'girl', *pert* 'pretty', *y ferch bert* 'the pretty girl'. (The *m* → *f* change, while part of lenition, is not so obviously related to our casual speech phenomena.)

Finno-Ugric languages show lenition (called 'gradation' in this case) in related forms of words. Estonian has three degrees of consonant quantity and in this case lenition tends to reduce a consonant by one degree: rääkida (to speak) ma räägin (I speak). (These consonants are both phonologically voiceless; the second is short.)

In other languages, lenition is simply a marker of phonological position (allophony): in Spanish and Breton (Dressler, 1975: 24), voiced intervocalic stops are realized as voiced fricatives or sometimes approximants. The second category is where English must be classified: lenition in casually spoken English is represented largely by decreased closure in obstruents, though tapping and its attendant intervocalic voicing could be thought of as weakening as well. The reduction in length of consonant clusters could be considered a type of quantity lenition such as found in Estonian, though it generally serves no grammatical function.

The examples above demonstrate cases where a phonological process is minor in English but major in another language. Dressler (1975: 228) points out that even within a given language the same processes often operate in 'allegro' (casual speech) as major rules and in lento (formal/citation form speech) as minor rules. This could be said to be true of some processes found in English, such as [st] simplification: the failure to pronounce spelled 't' in 'hasten', 'fasten' and 'Christmas' represents a minor exception, while its non-appearance in sequences such as 'last minute' and 'first place' is ubiquitous.

### 5.1.2  Historical phonology

It has often been observed that much historical linguistics has to be based on written language: there are no speakers of, say, Gothic upon whom to try one's reconstructions. Since written texts have a strong tendency to be conservative both in terms of preserving outdated pronunciations and in terms of being elevated in style, they normally are more representative of citation form than of unselfconscious casual speech.

Dressler (1975: 227) is one of the few to comment on the importance of casual speech to historical phonology:

> One of the greatest problems of historical phonology seems to me to be that practically nothing but lento forms are handed down . . . We therefore can see only the tip of the iceberg, so to speak, with respect to the then-available forms of the various styles of speech. Forms from less careful styles . . . are handed down only irregularly. Therefore, when one speaks of 'irregular' sound changes, it is only justified from the standpoint of lento phonology, which up to now has been practically the only topic in the history of language.

He gives the example (p. 229) of Latin *viginti* 'twenty' instead of the expected *vicinti*: a case, he believes of a single casual form penetrating into the standard language. 'The natural weakening process which is called lenition already existed in the Latin allegro style: only in the early Romance period did it come in as a lento sound change. However, the allegro process penetrated into single forms like *viginti* even in lento style and is therefore handed down as an irregular sound change in that word.'

Dressler advocates using not citation form and not the most reduced casual style as the basis for historical linguistics, but something in between.

### Variation: the crucible of change

Any natural language shows variation in pronunciation of both consonants and vowels at any time you choose. This variation is partly conditioned by environment and partly unconditioned in the sense that we have a good notion of where a variant will occur, but we cannot guarantee it. This is presumably an aspect of what Weinreich, Labov and Herzog (1968) call 'orderly heterogeneity'.

Further, one variant (in a particular environment) is regarded as more standard than the others and today's standard may not be the standard of tomorrow. E.g. pronunciation of intervocalic 'd' as [d] is standard in English and other pronunciations are regarded as nonstandard. On the other hand, what is spelled 'd' and was once presumably pronounced as [d] is now [ð] intervocalically in standard Danish. The fact that a continuant pronunciation of /d/ now exists intervocalically in casual English and that intervocalic lenition is a natural process suggests that one possible path for the standard English /d/ of tomorrow is in the direction of Danish (though the result would probably be alveolar instead of dental). But it is equally true that this path may not be taken: today's standard may be maintained, or another variant may become conventional. Tomorrow's standard will, however, predictably come from the set of today's pronunciations: for a completely novel variant to suddenly predominate would be very odd indeed.

Predictions about the sorts of variation one might expect in a particular system are possible: it is a recurrent theme in phonology that changes move in the direction of simplicity, naturalness, or unmarkedness. Bailey (1972: 36) says, 'the patterns of a language are the cumulative results of natural, unidirectional changes' and (p. 37) 'the directionality of natural change is from what is more marked to what is less marked.'

Stampe (1979) argues convincingly that marking conventions (i.e. calling a form 'marked' or 'unmarked') are superficial and unrevealing and that 'implicational laws, to the extent that they hold, are nothing more than empirical generalizations regarding the effects of natural processes' (p. 50). These processes, in his view, can thus be seen as opening avenues for sound change (see chapter 3), but, again, not deterministically.

Predictions about which variations will lead to change remain, at best, risky. Labov has contended that sound change in progress can be observed by studying language in its social context (Fasold, 1990: 227). He readily admits, however, that all change involves variability, but not all instances of variability involve change (Weinreich et al., 1968: 188).

It should not be forgotten that not all sound changes can be considered movements towards a more natural situation. Bailey (1973a: 131) points out that borrowing and 'typological adjustment' (Vennemann, 1972: 240) can be the basis of changes 'towards the marked case'. He cites the example of Hawaiian: when /k/ became a glottal stop in this language, /t/ changed to /k/ (arguably) to become maximally different from /p/, the only remaining stop. Since a system without /t/ is more marked than a system without /k/, this is change, in his terms, towards increased markedness. Bailey (p. 37) also discusses the apparent anomaly that whereas intervocalic lenition of stops is certainly common and is normally considered to be natural, it leads to the inclusion in the phonetic/allophonic inventory of unusual (marked) segments such as [β] and [x].

Vaissière (1998: 70) wittily observes that sound changes cannot be predicted, but they can almost always be given a number of more or less plausible explanations after they have been attested. She adds that not all phonological changes are related in an obvious way to observed continuous speech phenomena, citing raising of tense vowels, lowering of lax vowels, and fronting of back vowels as being among those historical processes not often observed as casual speech processes. Donegan (1993: 12) argues (independently of the casual speech process) that processes of this type are, however, natural, phonetically motivated, and, in a sense, predictable: 'Tensing increases color [palatality or labiality] and decreases sonority and Laxing increases sonority and decreases color. Tenseness thus makes vowels more susceptible to raising, and laxing makes vowels more susceptible to lowering . . .'

The pronunciation of casual speech thus cannot explain everything about historical phonological change. It can usefully be related to not only processes found in other languages but also to possible future standard pronunciations of one's own language. A hypothesis which deserves more attention is that that if a variation is found only in casual speech in one language, it will inevitably be found in other languages as part of the standard phonology. This is congruent with Bailey's contention (based on Decamp, 1971 and Elliot, Legum and Thompson, 1969) that linguistic variation patterns in an implicational manner (1972: 28) (though he did not mean interlinguistically).

### Collective unconscious?

Historical linguists have observed that the same change can occur (apparently independently) in several sibling languages after they have broken away from the parent. Latin *aurum*, for example, yielded Spanish, Italian *oro*, and French *or*. Based on this, some linguists have suggested that members of language families have internal tendencies towards particular changes which can be triggered by some unknown catalyst (Sapir's 'drift', Schultze's 'speech predisposition', cited in Dressler, 1975: 230). A much more likely explanation is that a pronunciation (here the one with [o]) was part of the vernacular system at the time these languages split off from the parent. The change then 'percolated up' from below to surface as a standard form in each of the sister languages.

We know, in fact, that [o] or [ɔ] for /au/ was variably present in vulgar Latin (Hall, 1968: 91; Smith, 1983: 903). While this might be seen as natural and for this reason alone within the scope of change for each of the sister languages, it is more than coincidence that it found its way into the standard system of each of them. As Dressler (p. 230) puts it, 'The appearance of independence is induced by the one-sided consideration of only lento phonology [in the parent language], since the sound change at issue can have been in existence as an allegro rule long before the separation. The problem of the causality of simultaneously-occurring changes is restricted thereby to the question of why a "cognate" allegro rule in separate languages will work its way more or less simultaneously into the lento systems.'

One can see the same slow emergence of vernacular forms with respect to loan phonology. 'If one accepts that the substratum languages influence the superstratum languages first at the popular level, therefore most in allegro styles, one can explain the paradoxical observation that substratum phenomena seem to show up for the first time very late in our documents, long after the extinction of the substratum in question' (Dressler, 1972: 229).

## 5.2 First and Second Language Acquisition

### 5.2.1 *First language acquisition*

It is often claimed that the speech used by caretakers to infants is especially clear and may be subconsciously designed to improve communication and possibly even promote language learning by providing a simple model. There is considerable evidence that (in some but not all cultures) child-directed speech differs from adult-directed speech in intonation, syntax, vocabulary, speed, and rate of repetition, but little work has been done on phonological input to young children.

Shockey and Bond (1980) recorded eight British mothers speaking to their two-to-four-year-old children and to adults in a relaxed home environment. They looked at phonological reductions such as final t-glottalling, ð-assimilation, and one type of cluster simplification (final -ts → s) and found that mothers used significantly more reduced forms to their children than they did to adults.

We have argued in chapter 2 that phonological reduction is, on the whole, not done consciously, so that being able to purposely vary the degree of reduction in different situations is unlikely. Yet phonological reduction appears to be part of the complex behaviour associated with talking to infants, at least in Anglo culture. Of course, the 'Idn't oo a pitty wittle beebee' stereotype of infant-directed speech is a gross exaggeration of what is found, but it captures the fact that reduced speech is informal and intimate. We hypothesized that mothers used it as a way of expressing solidarity and affection towards their young children.

We then asked how children acquire correct lexical representations if (as is often believed), the primary caretaker is the major language model. We concluded that the answer lies in the variability in the speech used by and to the caretaker. In the first place, speech directed by them to children is not uniform: our results showed that input from the caretaker does contain examples of unreduced forms. Secondly, simply because child-directed speech rarely contains citation forms does not ensure that the child is deprived of the opportunity to hear formal variants, both those used by the caretaker to other adults and those directed at the caretaker in the child's presence.

It thus seems likely that hearing a range of inputs allows children as well as adults to create a model of permissible variation in pronunciation and that casual forms are easily interpreted by children as affectively positive.

### 5.2.2   Second language acquisition

For a 19-year-old Dutch undergraduate who, after 6 years of English at a grammar school and after a whole year of studying English at a Dutch university, goes to England for the first time in his life . . . steps off the train, goes up to a porter and asks the way to Victoria bus station, it is a traumatic experience to find out that he does not understand a single word the porter says to him. (Koster, 1987: 1)

Most people who have lived in a foreign country empathize deeply with Koster's dismay: it was only after two years in Brazil that I could understand the speech of strangers in a bus queue, and even then I made mistakes.

Needless to say, there are many factors which contribute to understanding a foreign language. One obvious factor which does not seem to have received much attention in the literature is the connected speech processes outlined in chapter 2: especially if taught by non-native speakers of English, students are unlikely to have had significant contact with naturally reduced speech.

Brown (1977, 1996) uses this premise as a platform for her book *Listening to Spoken English.* Few attempts are made, she observes on her first page (1972), to teach English as spoken by native English speakers. Though many foreign visitors speak English reasonably comprehensibly, they cannot understand it. She cites an article in a 1971 English newspaper reporting that 'many overseas students are unable to understand English as spoken by university and college lecturers', sometimes to such an extent that they give up their course of studies. If this is to be remedied,

> The foreign student, then, is going to have to learn to abstract the message from a fairly reduced acoustic signal. He will not hear a string of explicitly articulated sounds which he can build into words and then sentences. He will hear an overall sound envelope with moments of greater and lesser prominence and will have to learn to make intelligent guesses, from all the clues available to him, about what the probable content of the message was and to revise this interpretation if necessary as one sentence follows another – in short, he has to learn to listen like a native speaker (p. 4).

Dressler (1975: 219) comments, 'Fast speech rules . . . are one of the most important parts of phonology in its application to . . . the teaching of foreign languages, where fast speech phonology has previously been neglected. This is because the allegro forms of the foreign language are not properly learned or taught or because the speaker erroneously applies allegro rules of the native language to foreign languages.' (Also see Dressler, 1971.)

Both Koster and I ask how native speakers and non-natives differ in their perception of connected speech. I have done a few pilot studies based on this question.

## Experiment 1

The first experimental sentence mentioned in chapter 4, 'The screen play didn't resemble the book at all', gated in stages of approximately 50 msec. (a total of 33 stimuli), was presented to 16 non-native speakers of English. A reminder of the phonetic transcription follows:

[ðəˈskɹĩmplɛɪdɪᵈn̩ɹɪzẽmbɫðəˈbʊkətˈɔɫ]

All subjects had studied at The University of Reading for at least one year, were surrounded (during the day, at least) with an English-speaking environment, and had had all of their lectures in English. Otherwise, there was little uniformity in this group of listeners: they came from different countries and had been in England for varying lengths of time.

The most obvious result was that only four of the sixteen listeners understood the sentence entirely correctly.

Working our way through the time course of the sentence, ten listeners first heard 'scream' but changed it to 'screen'. This change was much more spread out in time than in the case of the native speakers: five of the ten non-natives made the change as soon as the conditioning factor ([p]) appeared, the others during 'resemble' or 'all'.

Only four arrived at a correct interpretation of 'didn't', two of these during the phrase 'at all'.

## Experiment 2

The same gated sentence was presented to 16 native speakers of Hong Kong Cantonese, all young women studying to be teachers of English who had achieved a high score on an English proficiency test. They had more contact with each other than with native speakers of English, though their course was delivered in English.

The most striking feature of the results is that no one understood the entire sentence though some were able to capture its phonetic profile. Below is a subset of the answers. Interestingly, some of the Hong Kong teachers made the switch from 'scream' to 'screen' but were not able to use the derived information productively.

The screen played is at the bottom book of tall.
The screen played example of book at all.
The screen play thin reasonable book at top.
The screem played n ressembled of book at all.
The screen played isn't resemble the book at all.
The scrim plated resemble the booked at all.
The scream pladenn resemble the book at all.
The scream play dern resemble the book at all.
The screem played in resimple the book at all.

The last few subjects seem to have all the phonetic information they need to interpret the sentence correctly. We assume that a lack of familiarity with casual speech is a major factor in their lack of comprehension (though it has been pointed out that 'screenplay' is a rather unusual vocabulary item and this may well contribute significantly to its lack of recognition).

## Experiment 3

The second sentence used in my experiments in chapter 4, which is composed entirely of familiar vocabulary

[sʷɪʷəʷsˈkwaɪʔg ʊdfʌnæ̃ʧʊwɪɒnn̥əˈwɛdɨŋd̥θʉ]
So it was quite good fun, actually, on the wedding, though.

was presented in gated form to nine native speakers of Greek. Several of these had lived in England for over ten years, and two were married to native English speakers.

None of the listeners got the whole sentence correct. Only one (who attributed her perceptual expertise to long evenings of field work in the pub) recognized the first word, 'so'.

Of the eight who heard the stressed word 'quite', three were early perceivers, one recognized it at the end of 'fun' and one recognized it at the beginning of 'wedding'.

The two subjects with English spouses heard 'good fun' as it was being said. Two other subjects recognized 'fun' at its completion and one during the word 'on'. Four Greeks recognized 'wedding' (though two reported 'Reading', the town in which they live).

It will be remembered that this sentence was difficult for the native speakers, calling for considerable context before it could be interpreted. Not surprisingly, the Greek speakers, despite their long and frequent exposure to English, found it very difficult indeed.

## Discussion

In general, non-native speakers take longer than natives to interpret relaxed conversational input. They depend heavily on syntactico-semantic information to arrive at an understanding rather than using phonological context to disambiguate reductions. It appears that by and large they are not processing the language as it comes in, but rather taking in a relatively large amount of spoken language to process and thereby introducing a processing lag, much as predicted by Brown (1977) in the quotation above. Results by Truin (quoted in Koster, 1987: 33) bear this out: non-natives need more acoustic-phonetic information than natives for the recognition of isolated words. Koster's own results (p. 136) show that non-natives make more errors in identification of speech sounds and that they take longer to identify those that they get right.

Of course, gated speech cannot be regarded as equivalent to speech which is produced naturally as a communicative act in an appropriate situation, and one could argue that non-natives would have done better in a real-life situation (though Koster (p. 27) argues to the contrary, since gating allows subjects much more time for hypothesis testing, guessing and backtracking). But our gated stimuli were presented identically to native (chapter 4) and non-native speakers, and though the native speakers experienced some difficulty, they recognized the intended message much more easily than the non-natives.

Koster analyses very little natural conversational speech, but he joins Marslen-Wilson and Gaskell (see chapter 4) in looking at assimilation across word boundaries (sadly, one of the least interesting of casual speech reductions). He found (p. 142) that assimilation has a negative effect on non-native speech perception.

This is a strong argument for including perception of conversational speech in English courses for those planning to live in English-speaking countries and may even be an argument for explicit teaching of types of phonological reduction and where they are likely to occur. Koster (p. 143) disagrees with the latter: 'Letting foreign language students listen frequently to the spoken language with all the characteristics of connected speech is no doubt more important than familiarizing them with the theoretical aspects of, for instance, assimilation.'

First-language learners have intensive experience with a variety of different styles of speech and can thus subconsciously deduce the relationships between and among them (cf. Shockey and Bond, 1980). Examination of the second-language acquisition literature reveals very little direct concern with the importance of variability in phonological input. Gaies (1977) cites the increased use of repetition and the apparent simplifications which exist in speech to young children as possible sources of tailoring of input to second-language learners, but the paper itself focuses on syntax as input.

Literature on variation reflects interest in variation in the speech of the language learner rather than in the speech of the teacher or other model. Sato (1985), for example, looks at stylistic variation in the speech of a single young immigrant, but is not explicit as to the variation present in the target styles.

One study addresses the question from a purely *phonetic* standpoint (Pisoni and Lively, 1995). It considers the importance of variability of input to the second-language acquisition of new phonetic contrasts, and comes to the conclusion that high-variability training procedures (in which the contrast to be acquired is spoken by a variety of speakers in several different phonetic environments) promote the development of robust perceptual categories (p. 454). That is, sufficient evidence about the array of things which can be called phonetically 'same' in a second language promotes the creation of good perceptual targets, and targets which remain stable over time. 'In summary', they conclude, 'we suggest that the traditional approach to speech perception has been somewhat misguided with regard to the nature of the perceptual operations which occur when listeners process spoken language. Variability may not be noise. Rather, it appears to be informative to perception' (p. 455).

There is no reason that the same argument could not hold for phonological variability: exposure to a range of inputs which are phonetically different but phonologically the same will aid in overall comprehension of naturally-varying native speech. This is compatible with the notion discussed in chapter 3 that traces of each perceived token of a word remain in mental storage and can enlarge the perceptual target for that word.

Our experiments yield thought-provoking results, but they are only pilot studies and much more needs to be done. It will give greater insight (1) to control for age, nature of first and subsequent languages, and time abroad of the subjects, so as to determine the relative importance of each of these factors to perception of connected speech; (2) to use a much larger body of subjects; (3) to relate results for individuals to their score on English language proficiency examinations which are needed to enter university; and (4) to use sentences containing a much wider variety of conversational speech reductions.

As a postscript, whether teaching non-natives to *use* casual speech forms in their own speech is a good idea or not is a completely different question. Brown (1996: 60) recommends that the production of these forms should be reserved for the very advanced student.

## 5.3  Interacting with Computers

Insight into 'real speech' is fundamental for speech technology. While there may be no reluctance to accept this opinion amongst speech technologists, little progress has been made towards coming to grips with normal variation in pronunciation.

### 5.3.1  Speech synthesis

Naturalness in synthetic speech is a current concern, especially with respect to speech styles (e.g. Hirschberg and Swerts, 1998). It seems obvious that inclusion of casual speech processes in synthetic speech is a step in the right direction, but while it has been shown that casual speech forms can be generated using nonsegmental synthesis (Coleman, 1995), the use of casual speech processes in speech synthesis by rule has not, to my knowledge, been seriously considered, probably because casual speech is thought to be harder to understand than citation-form speech. As an advocate of the notion that reductions actually *add* information (about place in syllable, stress, following phonetic unit, communicative force, etc.) while possibly taking some away (segmental place and manner cues, for example), I would like to see systematic research into the effect of introducing the most frequent reduction processes into English synthetic speech. My prediction is that it will make the speech no less intelligible and will improve naturalness.

### 5.3.2  Speech recognition

Greenberg (2001) observes that historically there has been a tension between science and technology with respect to automatic recognition of spoken language, and I can report personally having heard disparaging remarks about the 'engineering approach' to speech/language from linguists and about the uselessness of linguists from computer scientists and engineers. Traditionally, technologists have used stochastic techniques and complex matching algorithms for recognizing speech, while linguists have recommended taking advantage of the regularities known to exist in spoken language, i.e. using acoustic/linguistic rules. (While casual speech rules can be said to be 'spelled out' in lexicons where all possible alternative pronunciations are included, there is no overt recognition of their presence.) Greenberg expresses optimism that these two points of view can be reconciled and that the goal of recognizing unscripted speech (which has remained distant despite half a century of earnest research) can eventually be reached.

He focuses (2001 and 1998) on a subset of just the sort of regularities we have observed in chapter 2, finding reason for optimism in the fact that while segment-based recognition is still as far away as ever, syllable-based recognition may be possible. He bases this on the apparent stability of the syllable, and especially of the consonantal syllable onset which, as we have observed, reduces far less frequently than the consonantal coda. He assumes that the fundamental difference between stressed and unstressed syllables in English can be useful (though he stands on the shoulders of other speech scientists in this, see Lea, 1980; Waibel, 1988). He also mentions the well-known fact that low-frequency and high-information words are less reduced than high-frequency, low-information ones (1998: 55), though how this is to be used in speech recognition is not made clear.

We have observed above that suprasegmental features of speech (fundamental frequency excursions, overall amplitude envelope, durational patterns of syllables) tend to be preserved despite casual speech reductions, and Greenberg's emphasis on stressed syllables suggests one way to take advantage of suprasegmental information. Hawkins and Smith (2001: 28) suggest that processing is driven by the temporal nature of the speech signal and discuss some systems where this is partially implemented (Boardman et al., 1999; Grossberg et al., 1997; Grossberg and Myers, 2000). They also recommend a focus on long-domain properties such as nasality, lip-rounding, and vowel-to-vowel coarticulation, in the spirit of the Prosodic approach mentioned in chapter 3.

Progress should be seen if a method can be devised to analyse input for suprasegmental patterns (much as humans appear to be doing in casual speech) in conjunction with stochastic techniques.

## 5.4   Summary

Casual speech reductions are a fact of life to phoneticians and phonologists, but to those who work in adjunct fields, some of which may not call for intensive training in pronunciation, they can be seen as trivial or deleterious. I argue here that a knowledge of normal pronunciation as it is used daily by native speakers is important not only for historical linguistics, comparative phonology, and language learning and teaching, but also for speech technology.

# Bibliography

Al-Tamimi Y. (2002) 'h' variation and phonological theory: evidence from two accents of English. PhD thesis, The University of Reading (England).

Anderson, A. H., Bader, M., Bard, E. G., Boyle, E., Doherty, G., Garrod, S., Isard, S., Kowtko, J., McAllister, J., Miller, J., Sotillo, C., Thompson, H. S. and Weinert, R. (1991) The H.C.R.C. Map Task Corpus. *Language and Speech*, 34, 351–66.

Anderson, J. M. and Ewen, C. J. (1980) Studies in dependency phonology. *Ludwigsburg Studies in Language and Linguistics*, 4.

Anderson, J. M. and Jones, C. (1977) *Phonological Structure and the History of English*. North Holland.

Anderson, S. (1981) Why phonology isn't natural. *Linguistic Inquiry*, 12, 493–539.

Anttila, A. (1997) Deriving variation from grammar. In F. Hinskens, R. van Hout and W. L. Wetzels (eds), *Variation, Change, and Phonological Theory*, John Benjamins.

Archambault, D. and Maneva, B. (1996) Devoicing in post-vocalic Canadian French obstruents. *Proceedings of the Fourth International Conference on Spoken Language Processing*, vol. 3, paper 834.

Archangeli, D. and Langendoen, D. T. (1997) *Optimality Theory: An Overview*. Blackwell.

Archangeli, D. (1988) Aspects of underspecification theory. *Phonology*, 5, 183–207.

Avery, P. and Rice, K. (1989) Segment structure and coronal underspecification. *Phonology*, 6, 179–200.

Bailey, C.-J. (1973a) *Variation and Linguistic Theory*. Center for Applied Linguistics, Arlington, Virginia.

Bailey, C.-J. (1973b) *New Ways of Analyzing Variation in English*. Georgetown University Press.

Bard, E. G., Shillcock, R. C. and Altmann, G. T. M. (1988) The recognition of words after their acoustic offsets in spontaneous speech: effects of subsequent context. *Perception and Psychophysics*, 44, 395–408.

Barlow, M. and Kemmer, S. (eds) (2000) *Usage-based Models of Language*. Stanford CSLI, 65–85.

Barry, M. (1984) Connected speech: processes, motivations, models. *Cambridge Papers in Phonetics and Experimental Linguistics*, 3 (no page numbers).

Barry, M. (1985) A palatographic study of connected speech processes. *Cambridge Papers in Phonetics and Experimental Linguistics*, 4 (no page numbers).

Barry, M. (1991) Assimilation and palatalisation in connected speech. Proceedings of the ESCA Workshop, Barcelona. 9.1–9.5.

Bates, S. (1995) Towards a Definition of Schwa: An Acoustic Investigation of Vowel Reduction in English. PhD Thesis, Edinburgh University.

Bauer, L. (1986) Notes on New Zealand English phonetics and phonology. *English World-Wide*, 7, 225–58.

Beckman, M. E. (1996) When is a syllable not a syllable? In T. Otake and A. Cutler (eds), *Phonological Structure and Language Processing*. Mouton de Gruyter.

Bladon, R. A. W. and Al-Bamerni, A. (1976) Coarticulation resistance in English /l/. *Journal of Phonetics*, 4, 137–50.

Boardman, I., Grossberg, S., Myers, C. W. and Cohen, M. (1999) Neural dynamics of perceptual order for variable-rate speech syllables. *Perception and Psychophysics*, 61, 1477–500.

Boersma, P. (1997) *Functional Phonology*. Holland Academic Graphics.

Bolozky, S. (1977) Fast speech as a function of tempo in natural generative phonology. *Journal of Linguistics*, 13, 217–38.

Borowski, T. and Horvath, B. (1997) L-Vocalisation in Australian English. In F. Hinskens, R. van Hout and W. L. Wetzels (eds), *Variation, Change and Phonological Theory*. John Benjamins, 101–24.

Browman, C. and Goldstein, L. (1986) Towards an articulatory phonology. *Phonology Yearbook*, 3, 219–52.

Browman, C. and Goldstein, L. (1990) Tiers in articulatory phonology, with some implications for casual speech. In John Kingston and Mary Beckman (eds), *Papers in Laboratory Phonology I*. Cambridge University Press, 341–76.

Browman, C. and Goldstein, L. (1992) Articulatory phonology: an overview. *Phonetica*, 49, 155–80.

Brown, G. (1977 and 1996) *Listening to Spoken English*. Pearson Education/Longman.

Brown, G., Anderson, A. H., Shillcock, R. and Yule, G. (1984) *Teaching Talk*. Cambridge University Press.

Bybee, J. (1999) Usage-based phonology. In M. Darnell, E. Moravcsik, M. Noonan, F; J. Newmeyer and Wheatley (eds), *Functionalism and Formalism in Linguistics, vol. 2: case studies*. John Benjamins, 211–42.

Bybee, J. (2000a) The phonology of the lexicon: evidence from lexical diffusion. In

Bybee, J. (2000b) Lexicalization of sound change and alternating environments. In M. Broe and J. Pierrehumbert (eds), *Papers in Laboratory Phonology V*. Cambridge University Press, 250–68.

Byrd, D. (1992) Perception of assimilation in consonant clusters: a gestural model. *Phonetica*, 49, 1–24.

Cedergren, H. J. and Sankoff, D. (1974) Variable rules: performance as a statistical reflection of competence. *Language*, 50, 333–55.

Cohn, A. (1993) Nasalisation in English: phonology or phonetics. *Phonology*, 10, 43–81.

Cole, R. and Jakimik. J. (1978) A model of speech perception. In R. Cole (ed.), *Production and Perception of Fluent Speech*. Lawrence Erlbaum, 133–63.

Coleman, J. S. (1992) The phonetic interpretation of headed phonological structures containing overlapping constituents. *Phonology*, 9, 1–42.

Coleman, J. S. (1994) Polysyllabic words in the YorkTalk synthesis system. In P. A. Keating (ed.), *Phonological Structure and Phonetic Form: Papers in Laboratory Phonology III*. Cambridge: Cambridge University Press, 293–324.

Coleman, J. S. (1995) Synthesis of connected speech. In L. Shockey (ed.), *The University of Reading Speech Research Laboratory Work in Progress*, no. 8, 1–12.

Comrie, B. (1987) *The World's Major Languages*. Routledge.

Cooper, A. M. (1991) Laryngeal and oral gestures in English /P,T,K/. *Proceedings of the 12th International Congress of Phonetic Sciences V*, 50–3.

Cruttenden, A. (2001) *Gimson's Pronunciation of English*. Arnold.

Cutler, A. (1995) Spoken word recognition and production. In J. Miller and P. Eimas (eds), *Speech, Language and Communication*. Academic Press.

Cutler, A. (1998) The recognition of spoken words with variable representations. In D. Duez (ed.), *Sound Patterns of Spontaneous Speech*. La Baume les Aix, 83–92.

Cutler, A. and Norris, D. (1988) The role of strong syllables in segmentation for lexical access. *Journal of Experimental Psychology: Human Perception and Performance*, 13, 113–21.

Cutler, A., Dahan, D. and van Donselaar, W. (1997) Prosody in the comprehension of spoken language: A literature review. *Language and Speech*, 40, 141–201.

Cutler, A., Mehler, J., Norris, D. and Segui, J. (1983) A language-specific comprehension strategy. *Nature*, 304, 159–60.

Dalby, J. M. (1984) Phonetic Structure of Fast Speech in American English. Ph.D. dissertation, Indiana University.

Daneman, M. and Merikle, P. M. (1996) Working memory and language comprehension: a meta-analysis. *Psychonomic Bulletin and Review*, 3, 422–33.

Davis, M. (2000) Lexical Segmentation in Spoken Word Recognition. Ph.D. thesis, Birkbeck College, University of London.

de Jong, K. (1998) Stress-related variation in the articulation of coda alveolar stops: flapping revisited. *Journal of Phonetics*, 26, 283–310.

Decamp, D. (1971) Towards a generative analysis of a post-creole speech continuum. In D. Hymes (ed.), *Pidginization and Creolization of Languages*. Cambridge University Press, 349–70.

Dilley, L., Shattuck-Hufnagel, S. and Ostendorf, M. (1997) Glottalizaton of word-initial vowels as a function of prosodic structure. *Journal of Phonetics*, 24, 423–44.

Dinnsen, D. (1980) Phonological rules and phonetic explanation. *Journal of Linguistics*, 16, 171–91.

Dirksen, A. and Coleman, J. S. (1994) All-prosodic synthesis architecture. *Proceedings of the Second ESCA/IEEE Workshop on Speech Synthesis*, September 12–15, 232–5.

Docherty, G. and Foulkes, P. (2000) Speaker, speech, and knowledge of sounds. In N. Burton-Roberts P. Carr and G. Docherty (eds), *Phonological Knowledge*. Oxford University Press, 105–29.

Docherty, G. and Fraser, H. (1993) On the relationship between acoustics and electropalatographic representations of speech. In L. Shockey (ed.), *University of Reading Speech Research Laboratory, Work in Progress*, no. 7, 8–25.

Donegan, P. (1993) Rhythm and vocalic drift in Munda and Mon-Khmer. *Linguistics of the Tibeto-Burman Area*, 16, 1–43.

Donegan, P. and Stampe, D. (1979) The study of natural phonology. In D. A. Dinnsen (ed.), *Current Approaches to Phonological Theory*. Indiana University Press, 126–73.

Dressler, W. U. (1975) Methodisches zu Allegro-Regeln. In W. U. Dressler and F. V. Mares (eds), *Phonologica 1972*. Wilhelm Fink, 219–34. (A translation of the article appears on the website associated with this book.)

Dressler, W. U. (1984) Explaining natural phonology. *Phonology Yearbook*, 1, 29–51.

Elliot, D., Legum, S. and Thompson, S. A. (1969) Syntactic variation as linguistic data. *Chicago Linguistic Society*, 5, 52–9.

Fabricius, A. H. (2000) T-Glottalling: Between Stigma and Prestige. Ph.D. thesis, Copenhagen Business School.

Farnetani, E. and Recasens, D. (1996) Coarticulation in recent speech production theory. *Quaderni del Centro di Studi per le Ricerche di Fonetica*, 15, 3–46.

Fasold, R. (1990) *The Sociolinguistics of Language*. Blackwell.

Firbas, J. (1992) *Functional Sentence Perspective in Written and Spoken Discourse*. Cambridge University Press.

Firth, J. R. (1957) Sounds and prosodies. In *Papers in Linguistics 1934–1951*. Oxford University Press, 121–38.

Fokes, J. and Bond, Z. S. (1993) The elusive/illusive syllable. *Phonetica*, 50, 102–23.

Foley, J. (1977) *Foundations of Theoretical Phonology*. Cambridge University Press.

Fougeron, C. and Keating, P. (1997) Articulatory strengthening at edges of prosodic domains. *Journal of the Acoustical Society of America*, 101, 3728–40.

Fowler, A. (1991) How early phonological development might set the stage for phoneme awareness. In S. Brady and D. P. Shankweiler (eds), *Phonological Processes in Literacy*. Lawrence Erlbaum, 97–118.

Fowler, C. A. (1985) Current perspectives on language and speech production: a critical review. In R. Daniloff (ed.), *Speech Science*. Taylor and Francis, 193–278.

Fowler, C. A. (1988) Differential shortening of repeated content words produced in various communicative contexts. *Language and Speech*, 31, 307–19.

Fowler, C. A. and Housum, J. (1987) Talkers' signalling of 'new' and 'old' words in speech. *Journal of Memory and Language*, 26, 489–504.

Fox, R. and Terbeek, D. (1977) Dental flaps, vowel duration, and rule ordering in American English. *Journal of Phonetics*, 527–34.

Fraser, H. (1992) *The Subject of Speech Perception: an analysis of the philosophical foundations of the information-processing model*. Macmillan.

Frauenfelder, U. and Lahiri, A. (1989) Understanding words and word recognition. In W. Marslen-Wilson (ed.), *Lexical Representation and Process*, MIT, 319–39.

Frazier, L. (1987) Structure in auditory word recognition. *Cognition*, 25, 262–75.

Fudge, E. (1967) The nature of phonological primes. *Journal of Linguistics*, 3, 1–36.

Fudge, E. and Shockey, L. (1998) The Reading database of syllable structure. In J. Nerbonne (ed.), *Linguistic Databases*. CSLI Publications, ‾93–102.

Gaies, S. (1977) The nature of linguistic input in formal second language learning: linguistic and communicative strategies in ESL teachers' classroom language in Brown, H. D., Yorio, C. A., & Crymes, R. H. (Eds.), *Teaching and Learning English as a Second Language: Trends in research and practice*, Washington, DC: TESOL., 204–12.

Gaskell, M. G. (2001) Lexical ambiguity resolution and spoken-word recognition: bridging the gap. *Journal of Memory and Language*, 44, 325–49.

Gaskell, M. G. and Marslen-Wilson, W. D. (1998) Mechanisms of phonological inference in speech perception. *Journal of Experimental Psychology, Human Perception and Performance*, 24, 380–96.

Gaskell, M. G., Hare, M. and Marslen-Wilson, W. D. (1995) A connectionist model of phonological representation in speech perception. *Cognitive Science*, 19, 407–39.

Godfrey, J. J., Holliman, E. C. and McDaniel, J. (1992) SWITCHBOARD: Telephone speech corpus for research and development. IEEE ICASSP 1: 517–20.

Goldringer, S. D. (1997) Words and voices: perception and production in an episodic lexicon. In K. Johnson and J. Mullennix (eds), *Talker Variability in Speech Processing*. Academic Press, 33–66.

Goldsmith, J. (1990) *Autosegmental and Metrical Phonology*. Blackwell.

Greenberg, J. (1969) Some methods of dynamic comparison in linguistics. In J. Puhvel (ed.), *Substance and Structure of Language*. Center for Research in Languages and Linguistics, 147–204

Greenberg, S. (1998) Speaking in shorthand – a syllable-centric perspective for understanding pronunciation variation. In H. Strik, J. M. Kessens and M. Wester (eds), *Proceedings of the ESCA workshop on Modelling Pronunciation Variation for Automatic Speech Recognition*. European Speech Communication Association, 47–56.

Greenberg, S. (2001) From here to utility: melding phonetic insight with speech technology. Proceedings of the 7th European Conference on Speech Communication and Technology, (Eurospeech-2001).

Greenberg, S. and Fosler-Lussier, E. (2000) The uninvited guest: information's role in guiding the production of spontaneous speech. Proceedings of the CREST workshop on Models of Speech Production: Motor Planning and Articulatory Modelling, Kloster Seeon, Germany, May 1–4.

Grosjean, F. (1980) Spoken word recognition processes and the gating paradigm. *Perception and Psychophysics*, 28, 267–83.

Grosjean, F. (1985) The recognition of words after their acoustic offset: evidence and implications. *Perception and Psychophysics*, 38, 299–310.

Grossberg, S. and Myers, C. W. (2000) The resonant dynamics of speech perception: interword integration and duration-dependent backwards effects. *Psychological Review*, 4, 735–67.

Grossberg, S., Boardman, I. and Cohen, M. (1997) Neural dynamics of variable-rate speech categorization. *Journal of Experimental Psychology: Human Perception and Performance*, 23, 481–503.

Guy, G. (1997) Competence, performance, and the Generative Grammar of variation. In F. Hinskens, R. van Hout and W. L Wetzels (eds) *Variation, Change, and Phonological Theory*. John Benjamins, 125–43.

Hall, R. Jr. (1968) *An Essay on Language*. Chilton Books.

Hardcastle, W. J. and Barry, W. J. (1985) Articulatory and perceptual factors in /l/ vocalisation in English. *University of Reading Phonetics Laboratory Work in Progress no. 5*, 31–44.

Harris, J. H. (1969) *Spanish Phonology*. MIT Press.

Hawkins, S. and Smith, R. (2001) Polysp: a polysystematic, phonetically-rich approach to speech understanding. *Journal of Italian Linguistics (Revista di Linguistica)*, 13, 99–108.

Helgason, P. (1991) On Coarticulation and Connected Speech Processes in Icelandic. MA thesis: University of Reading. (Published in 1993 by the Institute of Linguistics, University of Iceland.)

Helgason, P. (1996) Lenition in German and Icelandic. In A. Simpson and M. Pätzold (eds), *Institut fur Phonetik un digitale Sprachverarbeitung Arbeitsberichte*, 31, Universitat Kiel, 219–26.

Hertrich, I. and Ackermann, H. (1995) Coarticulation in slow speech: durational and spectral analysis. *Language and Speech*, 38, 159–87.

Hirschberg, J. and Swerts, M. (1998) Prosody and conversation. *Language and Speech*, 41, 3–4.

Holmes, J. (1994) New Zealand Flappers: An Analysis of T-Voicing in New Zealand English. *English World-Wide*, 15, 195–224.

Holst, T. and Nolan, F. (1995a) [s]-[S] Assimilation across a word boundary: is the citation form still lurking? In L. Shockey (ed.), *Reading University Speech Research Laboratory Work in Progress*, 8, 40–52.

Holst, T. and Nolan, F. (1995b) The influence of syntactic structure on [s]- [S] assimilation. In B. Connell and A. Arvaniti (eds), *Papers in Laboratory Phonology IV*. Cambridge University Press, 315–33.

Hooper, J. B. (1976) *An Introduction to Natural Generative Phonology.* Academic Press.

Howes, D. (1967) Equilibrium theory of word frequency distributions. *Psychonometric Bulletin,* 1, 18.

Jaeger, J. (1978) Speech aerodynamics and phonological universals. Proceedings of the annual meeting of the Berkeley Linguistics Society 4, 311–29.

Jakobson, R. and Halle, M. (1968) Phonology in relation to phonetics. In B. Malmberg (ed.), *Manual of Phonetics.* North Holland, 411–49.

Jannedy, S. (1994) High vowel devoicing in Turkish. ASA Meeting, Austin, http:www.auditory.org/asamtgs/asa94aus/4pSP/4pSPb.html

Johnson, K. and Mullennix, J. (eds) (1997) *Talker Variability in Speech Processing.* Academic Press.

Jun, S.-A. and Beckman, M. (1994) Distribution of devoiced high vowels in Korean. In Proceedings of the International Conference on Spoken Language Processing, volume 2, 479–82.

Jusczyk, P. (1997) *The Discovery of Spoken Language* MIT Press.

Jusczyk, P. (1999) How infants begin to extract words from speech. *Trends in Cognitive Science,* 3, 323–8.

Kager, R. (1999) *Optimality Theory.* Cambridge University Press.

Kaisse, E. M. (1985) Connected Speech: The Interaction of Syntax and Phonology. Academic Press.

Keating, P. (1997) Word-initial vs word-final consonant articulation. Poster, 134th Acoustical Society of America Meeting, San Diego. *Journal of the Acoustical Society of America,* 102, 3094(A).

Keating, P. (1988) The phonetics/phonology interface. In F. J. Newmeyer (ed.), *Linguistics: The Cambridge Survey.* Cambridge University Press, 281–302.

Kelly, J. and Local, J. K. (1986) Long-domain resonance patterns in English. Proceedings of the IEE Speech Input/Output Conference, 77–82.

Kelly, J. and Local, J. K. (1989) *Doing Phonology.* Manchester University Press.

Kerswill, P. (1985) A sociophonetic study of connected speech processes in Cambridge English. *Cambridge Papers in Phonetics and Experimental Linguistics,* 4 (no page numbers).

Kerswill, P. (1995) Phonological convergence in dialect contact: evidence from citation forms. *Language Variation and Change,* 7, 195–208.

Kerswill, P. and Wright, S. (1989) Electropalatography in the study of connected speech processes. *Clinical Linguistics and Phonetics,* 3, 49–57.

Kisseberth, C. (1970) On the functional unity of phonological rules. *Linguistic Inquiry*, 1, 291–306.

Kohler, K. (1992) Gestural reorganization in connected speech: a functional viewpoint on 'articulatory phonology'. *Phonetica*, 49, 205–11.

Koster, C. J. (1982) De T T W op het juiste pad? Een pad-analyse. *Toegepaste Taalwetenschap in Artikelen*, 14, 109–16.

Koster, C. J. (1987) *Word Recognition in Foreign and Native Language*. Foris.

Krull, D. (1987) Second formant locus patterns as a measurement of consonant-vowel coarticulation. *PERILUS* (Phonetic Experimental Research at the Institute of Linguistics, University of Stockholm), 5, 43–61.

Krull, D. (1989) Second formant locus patterns and consonant-vowel coarticulation in spontaneous speech. *PERILUS*, 9, 87–108.

Labov, W. (1969) Contraction, deletion, and inherent variability of the English copula. *Language*, 45, 715–62.

Labov, W. (1997) Resyllabification. In F. Hinskens, R. van Hout and W. L. Wetzels (eds), *Variation, Change, and Phonological Theory*. John Benjamins, 145–802.

Ladefoged, P. (1983) Out of chaos comes order: physical, biological, and structural patterns in phonetics. In M. van den Broeke and A. Cohen (eds), *Proceedings of the 10th International Congress of Phonetic Sciences*, 83–96.

Lahiri, A. and Marslen-Wilson, W. (1991) The mental representation of lexical form. *Cognition*, 38, 245–94.

Langendoen, T. (1968) *The London School of Linguistics*. MIT Press.

Lass, R. (1984) *Phonology*. Cambridge University Press.

Lea, W. (1980) Prosodic aids to speech recognition. In W. A. Lea (ed.), *Trends in Speech Recognition*. Prentice-Hall, 166–205.

Lehiste, I. (1970) *Suprasegmentals*. MIT Press.

Lehiste, I. (1972) The timing of utterances and linguistic boundaries. *Journal of the Acoustical Society of America*, 51, 2018–24.

Liberman, M. (1975) The Intonation System of English, Dissertation, MIT.

Lieberman, P. (1970) Some effects of semantic and grammatical context on the production and perception of speech. *Language and Speech*, 6, 172–87.

Lindblom, B. (1963) On vowel reduction. Royal Institute of Technology, Stockholm, report no. 29.

Lindblom, B. (1964) Articulatory activity in vowels. *STL/QPSR* 2. Royal Institute of Technology, Stockholm Sweden, 1–5.

Lindblom, B. (1990) Phonetic variation: a sketch of the H&H Theory. In W. J. Hardcastle and A. Marchal (eds), *Speech Production and Speech Modelling*. Kluwer, 403–39.

Local, J. and Lodge, K. R. (1996) Another travesty of representation: phonological representation and phonetic interpretation of ATR harmony in Kalenjin. *York Papers in Linguistics*, 17, 77–117.

Local, J. and Ogden, R. (1997) A model of timing for nonsegmental phonological structure. In J. P. H. van Santen, R. W. Sproat, J. P. Olive and J. Hirschberg (eds), *Progress in Speech Synthesis*. Springer.

Lodge, K. R. (1981) Dependency phonology and English consonants. *Lingua*, 54, 19–39.

Lodge, K. R. (1984) *Studies in the Phonology of Colloquial English*. Croon Helm.

Lodge, K. R. (1992) Assimilation, deletion paths and underspecification. *Journal of Linguistics*, 28, 13–52.

Lodge, K. R. (1993) Underspecification, polysystemicity, and nonsegmental representations in phonology: an analysis of Malay. *Linguistics*, 31, 475–519.

Lodge, K. R. (1995) Kalenjin phonology and morphology: A further example of underspecification and non-destructive phonology. *Lingua*, 96, 29–43.

Lodge, K. R. (1997) Domains of assimilation: alveolars and velars in English. *Journal of the International Phonetic Association*, 27, 57–64.

Lovins, J. B. (1978) 'Nasal reduction' in English syllable codas. In *Proceedings of the Chicago Linguistic Society*, 14, 241–53.

Luce, P. A. (1986) Neighborhoods of Words in the Mental Lexicon. PhD thesis, Indiana University.

Lundberg, L., Olofsson, A. and Wall, S. (1980) Reading and spelling skills in the first school year predicted from phonemic awareness skills in kindergarten. *Scandinavian Journal of Psychology*, 21, 159–73.

Malecot, A. and Lloyd, P. (1968) The /t/:/d/ distinction in American alveolar flaps. *Lingua*, 19, 264–72.

Mann, V. A. (1991) Are we taking too narrow a view of the conditions for development of phonological awareness? In D. P. Shankweiler and S. Brady (eds), *Phonological Processes in Literacy*. Lawrence Erlbaum, 55–64.

Manuel, S. (1987) Acoustic and perceptual consequences of vowel-to-vowel coarticulation in three Bantu languages. PhD dissertation, Yale University.

Manuel, S. (1990) The role of contrast in limiting vowel-to-vowel coarticulation in different languages. *Journal of the Acoustical Society of America*, 88, 1286–98.

Manuel, S. (1991) Recovery of 'deleted' schwa. *PERILUS* 14, Papers from the Symposium on Current Phonetic Research Paradigms: Implications for Speech Motor Control, University of Stockholm Institute of Linguistics, 115–18.

Manuel, S. (1995) Speakers nasalise /ð/ after /n/, but listeners still hear /ð/. *Journal of Phonetics*, 23, 453–76.

Marslen-Wilson, W. and Welsh, A. (1978) Processing interactions and lexical access during word recognition in continuous speech. *Cognitive Psychology*, 10, 29–83.

Marslen-Wilson, W., Nix, A. and Gaskell, G. (1995) Phonological variation in lexical access. *Language and Cognitive Processes*, 10, 285–308.

Massaro, D. W. (1987) *Speech Perception by Ear and Eye*. Lawrence Erlbaum.

McClelland, J. L. and Elman, J. L. (1986) Interactive processes in speech perception: the TRACE model. In J. L. McClelland and D. E. Rumelhart, *Parallel Distibuted Processing*. MIT Press, 58–121.

Merrit, D. L. (1984 [1910]) The Pelican. In E. O. Parrot, *The Penguin Book of Limericks*. Penguin Books, 39.

Mullennix, J. W., Pisoni, D. B. and Martin, C. S. (1989) Some effects of talker variability on spoken word recognition. *Journal of the Acoustical Society of America*, 85, 379–90.

Nathan, G. (1988) Variability in constraint ranking as a puzzle for OT. Mid-Continent Workshop on Phonology (McWOP4), Ann Arbor, October.

Nespor, M. and Vogel, I. (1986) *Prosodic Phonology*. Foris.

Nolan, F. (1986) The implication of partial assimilation and incomplete neutralisation. *Cambridge Papers in Phonetics and Experimental Linguistics*, 5 (no page numbers).

Nolan, F. (1992) The descriptive role of segments: evidence from assimilation. In Docherty, G. and Ladd D. R. (eds), *Papers in Laboratory Phonology II*, 261–80.

Nolan, F. (1996) Overview of English connected speech processes. In A. Simpson and M. Pätzold (eds), *Sound Patterns of Connected Speech: Description, Models, and Explanation*, Arbeitsberichte (AIPUK) nr 31, Institute für Phonetik und digitale Sprachverarbeitung. Universität Kiel.

Nolan, F. and Cobb, H. (1994) Connected speech processes in Cambridge English: an evaluative experiment. In G. Melchers and N.-L. Johannesson (eds), *Nonstandard Varieties of Language*. Almquist and Wiksell, 146–58.

Nolan, F. and Kerswill, P. E. (1990) The description of connected speech processes. In S. Ramsaran (ed.), *Studies in the Pronunciation of English*, Routledge, 295–316.

Nolan, F., Holst, T. and Kühnert, (1996) Modelling [s] to [S] assimilation in English. *Journal of Phonetics*, 24, 113–37.

Nolan, F., Wright, S. and Kerswill, P. (1991) End of EPSRC Award Report R000231056.

Norris, D. (1994) Shortlist: a connectionist model of continuous speech recognition. *Cognition*, 52, 189–234.

Ogden, R. (1999) A declarative account of strong and weak auxiliaries in English. *Phonology*. 16, 55–92.

Ohala, J. J. (1975) A mathematical model of speech aerodynamics. In G. Fant (ed.), *Speech Communication II, Speech Production and Synthesis by Rules*. Almqvist and Wiksell, 65–72.

Ohala. J. J. (1990) There is no interface between phonology and phonetics: a personal view. *Journal of Phonetics*, 18, 153–71.

Paradis, C. and Prunet, J.-F. (1989) On coronal transparency. *Phonology*, 6, 317–48.

Paradis, C. and Prunet, J.-F. (1991) *The Special Status of Coronals: Internal and External Evidence*. Academic Press.

Patterson, D. and Connine, C. (in press) A corpus analysis of variant frequency in American English flap production. *Journal of Phonetics*.

Perkell, J. and Klatt, D. (eds) (1986) *Invariance and Variability in Speech Processes*. Erlbaum.

Pickett, J. M. and Pollack, I. (1963) Intelligibility of excerpts from conversation. *Language and Speech*, 6, 165–71.

Pierrehumbert, J. (1994) Knowledge of Variation, Papers from the Parasession on Variation. *Chicago Linguistic Society*, 232–56.

Pisoni, D. and Lively, S. (1995) Variability and invariance in speech perception. In W. Strange (ed.), *Speech Perception and Linguistic Experience*. York Press, 433–62.

Port, R. F. (1981) Linguistic timing factors in combination. *JASA*, 69, 262–74.

Price, P. J. (1980) Sonority and syllabicity: acoustic correlates of perception,. *Phonetica*, 37, 327–43.

Prince, A. and Smolensky, P. (1993) Optimality Theory: Constraint Interaction in Generative Grammar. MS, Rutgers University and University of Colorado.

Roach, P., Sergeant, P. and Miller, D. (1992) Syllabic consonants at different speaking rates: a problem for automatic speech recognition. *Speech Communication*, 11, 475–9.

Roca, I. and Johnson, G. (1999) *A Course in Phonology*. Blackwell.

Rodgers, J. (1999) Vowel devoicing in English. PhD thesis, University of Cambridge.

Sato, C. (1985) Task variation in interlanguage phonology. In S. Gass and C. Madden (eds), *Input and Second Language Acquisition,*. Newbury House, 181–96.

Shankweiler, D. and Crain, S. (1986) Language mechanisms and reading disorder: A modular approach. *Cognition*, 24, 139–68.

Shillcock, R., Bard, E. and Spensley, F. (1988) Some prosodic effects on human word recognition in continuous speech. Proceedings of SPEECH '88, 7th FASE Symposium, 819–26.

Shockey, L. (1974) Phonetic and phonological properties of connected speech. *Ohio State Working Papers in Linguistics*, 17, 1–143.

Shockey, L. (1978) Perceptual test of a phonological rule. *Haskins Laboratories Quarterly Progress Report*, June, 147–50.

Shockey, L. (1987) Rate and reduction: some preliminary evidence. In R. Channon and L. Shockey (eds), *In Honor of Ilse Lehiste*. Foris, 217–24.

Shockey, L. (1991) EPG of connected speech. *Proceedings of the XIIth International Congress of Phonetic Sciences*. Aix-en-Provence, 10–13.

Shockey, L. and Bond, Z. S. (1980) Phonological processes in speech addressed to children. *Phonetica*, 37, 267–74.

Shockey, L. and Farnetani, E. (1992) EPG of spontanteous speech in English and Italian. Proceedings of the International Conference on Spoken Language Processing, Banff, Alberta, Canada, October, 667–70.

Shockey, L. and Gibbon, F. (1992) 'Stopless stops' in connected English. *Reading Speech Research Laboratory Work in Progress*, 7, 1–7.

Shockey, L. and Watkins, A. (1995) Reconstruction of base forms in perception of casual speech. In K. Elenius and P. Branderud (eds), *Proceedings of the 13th International Congress of Phonetic Sciences*. Stockholm, 588–91.

Shockey, L., Spelman Miller, K. and Wichmann, A. (1994) Focus: linking meaning and phonology. In P. Bosch and R. van der Sandt (eds), *Focus and Natural Language Processing*. IBM Deutschland Informationssystem GmbH Scientific Centre, Working Paper 8, 175–84.

Simpson, A. (1992) Casual speech rules and what the phonology of connected speech might really be like. *Linguistics*, 30, 535–48.

Skoyles, J. R. (2001) The two paradigms of speech perception: 'reading' vs 'soup'. http://www.users.globalnet.co.uk/~skoyles/speech.html

Smith, C. (1983) Vulgar Latin in Roman Britain: epigraphic evidence. In H. Temporini and W. Haase (eds), *Aufstieg und Niedergang Der Römischen Welt*. de Gruyter, 139–68.

Sotillo, C. F. (1997) Phonological reduction and intelligibility in task-oriented dialogue. PhD thesis, University of Edinburgh.

Stampe, D. (1973) On chapter nine. In M. Kenstowicz and C. W. Kisseberth (eds), *Issues in Phonological Theory*. Mouton, 44–52.

Stampe, D. (1979) *A Dissertation on Natural Phonology*. Chicago University Press.

Stampe, D. (1987) On phonological representations. In W. U. Dressler, H. C. Luschusky, O. E. Pfeiffer and J. R. Rennison (eds), *Phonologica 1984*. Cambridge University Press, 287–99.

Stone, M. and Hamlet, S. (1982) Variations in jaw and tongue gestures observed during the production of unstressed /d/s and flaps. *Journal of Phonetics*, 10, 401–15.

Sussman, H. M. (1991) An investigation of locus equations as a source of relational invariance for stop place categorization. PERILUS XIV, Papers from the Symposium on Current Phonetic Research Paradigms: Implications for Speech Motor Control. University of Stockholm Institute of Linguistics, 89–92.

Thompson, H. (1991) Chart parsing for loosely coupled parallel systems. In M. Tomita (ed.), *Current Issues in Parsing Technologies*. MIT Press, 231–41.

Trubetzkoy, N. I. (1969 [1939]) *Principles of Phonology*. Trans. C. Baltaxe, University of California Press. (Originally published (1939) as *Grundzuge der Phonologie*, Travaux du Cercle Linguistique de Prague 7.)

Truin, P. G. M. (1981) Herkenning van fragmenten van gesproken Nederlandse woorden door Nederlanders en niet-Nederlanders. *Toegepaste Taalwetenschap in Artikelen*, 9, 170–82.

Tunmer, W. E. and Rohl, M. (1991) Phonological awareness and reading acquisition. In D. J. Sawyer and B. J. Fox (eds), *Phonological Awareness in Reading*. Springer-Verlag, 1–30.

Turk, A. (1992) The American English flapping rule and the effect of stress on stop consonant durations. Working Papers of the Cornell Phonetics Laboratory 7, 103–33.

Vaissière, J. (1998) Synchronic variations, historical sound changes, and a suprasegmental framework. In D. Duez (ed.), *Sound Patterns of Spontaneous Speech (SPOSS)*. Laboratoire Parole et Langage, University of Aix en Provence, 69–82.

Vaux, B. (2000) Flapping in English. Linguistic Society of America paper, Chicago, http://icg.harvard.edu/~ling80/assignments/flap.pdf

Venemann, T. (1972) Sound change and markedness theory: on the history of the German consonant system. In R. P. Stockwell and R. K. S., Macauley, *Linguistic Change and Generative Theory*. Indiana University Press, 230–74.

Waibel, A. (1988) *Prosody in Speech Recognition*. Pitman.

Wang, W. (1977) *The Lexicon in Phonological Change*. Mouton, The Hague.

Warner, N. (1999) The relationship between syllable structure and speech perception. Fourth Holland Institute of Linguistics Phonology Conference, Leiden, January, http://wwwleidenuniv.nl/hil/confs/hilp4/warner.htm

Warren, R. M. (1970) Perceptual restoration of missing speech sounds. *Science*, 167, 392–3.

Warren, R. M. (1999) *Auditory Perception: A New Analysis and Synthesis.* Cambridge University Press.

Warren, R. M. and Obusek, C. J. (1971) Speech perception and phonemic restorations. *Perception and Psychophysics*, 12, 358–62.

Weil, S. (2001) Foreign-accented speech: adaptation and generalization. MA dissertation, The Ohio State University.

Weinreich, U., Labov, W. and Herzog, M. (1968) Empirical foundations for a theory of language change. In W. P. Lehmann and Y. Malkiel (eds), *Directions for Historical Linguistics.* University of Texas Press, 95–188.

Wells, J. C. (1982) *Accents of English.* Cambridge University Press.

Whalen, D. H. (1990) Coarticulation is largely planned. *Journal of Phonetics*, 3–35.

Whorf, B. L. (1941) The relation of habitual thought and behavior to language. In L. Spier (ed.), *Language, in Culture and Personality, Essays in Memory of Edward Sapir.* Sapir Memorial Publication Fund, 134–59.

Wright, S. (1986) The interaction of sociolinguistic and phonetically-conditioned CSPs in Cambridge English: auditory and electropalatographic evidence. *Cambridge Papers in Phonetics and Experimental Linguistics* 5 (no page numbers).

Wright, S. (1989) The effects of style and speaking rate in /l/-vocalisation. In Local Cambridge English, York Papers in Linguistics 18, 1989, 355–65.

Zee, E. (1990) Vowel devoicing in Shanghai. *Linguistics Abroad*, 3, 19–34.

Zue, V. W. and Laferriere, M. (1979) An acoustic study of medial /t,d/ in American English, *Journal of the Acoustical Society of America*, 66, 1030–50.

Zwicky, A. (1972a) Note on a phonological hierararchy in English. In R. P. Stockwell and R. K. S. Macaulay (eds), *Linguistic Change and Generative Theory.* Indiana University Press, 275–301.

Zwicky, A., (1972b) On casual speech. In P. M. Peranteau, J. W. Levi and G. C. Phares (eds), *Papers from the Eighth Regional Meeting of the Chicago Linguistic Society*, 607–15.

# Index